TOMMY McLEAN

TOMMY McLEAN

FOOTBALL IN THE BLOOD

MY AUTOBIOGRAPHY

WITH PAUL SMITH

BLACK & WHITE PUBLISHING

First published 2013
by Black & White Publishing Ltd
29 Ocean Drive, Edinburgh EH6 6JL

1 3 5 7 9 10 8 6 4 2   13 14 15 16

ISBN: 978 1 84502 704 9

A CIP catalogue record for this book is available from the British Library.

Typeset by RefineCatch Ltd, Bungay, Suffolk
Printed and bound by ScandBook AB, Sweden

To Beth and Lorna – my winning team

ACKNOWLEDGEMENTS

So many people have had a part to play in my life in so many different ways and I must take the opportunity to acknowledge at least some of those who have helped me along the way.

My thoughts turn firstly to those who are no longer here to share the stories and memories of some of the most important chapters in my life. I would like to thank my late parents for their unstinting support when I chose to pursue a career in football. My mother would have preferred me to have something more secure at my back but eventually gave her blessing. I will always be grateful to my father for his encouragement and support, especially in the early days when he helped shape the good habits that stayed with me throughout my career. I have had the honour of working with some wonderful characters and incredible professionals, none more so than those who have sadly passed away. The loss of Davie Cooper, Phillip O'Donnell, Paul McGrillen and Jamie Dolan left a huge void in Scottish football. Each was a credit to their family and I consider it a real privilege to have been part of their lives.

Returning to those who are still at the centre of my life, my thanks go to my wife, Beth, and daughter, Lorna, for keeping me fully focussed on the important things in life. Although I have been fortunate to have won many trophies and medals in football, the biggest and most important prize I have ever been given was when Lorna was born in November 1991. I met Beth at school and she knew at an early age how much football meant to me, being a constant support when the hard decisions had to be made. She is my rock and helps keep me grounded.

My brothers, Willie and Jim, have also always been there for me – not least when the going got tough. My appreciation goes to them for teaching me the game and, in particular, for imparting the coaching and management side of professional football which gave me so many good times.

Writing this book provided a wonderful opportunity to look back over those occasions and bring them back to life, a process I enjoyed immensely. My thanks go to Paul Smith for his dedicated work on this book, which was a pleasure to be involved with from start to finish, and the team at Black & White Publishing for their faith in the project.

Too many others to mention have had a major influence on me, inside and outside of football, and deserve enormous credit. I hope they know who they are.

Without all the people who have supported me in so many different ways, the story of my life would have been far less eventful and nowhere near as enjoyable.

CONTENTS

1

TEARS AND TRIUMPH

I have always believed that to truly appreciate the highs you must have experienced the lows. For me, all of those emotions came crashing together in a period that has shaped my life since and made me look at the years leading up to that time in a very different light.

It was 1991, a year memorable for so many reasons. For football followers the instant association is the Scottish Cup, *that* final against Dundee United and the success that meant so much for Motherwell. For my brothers and our family, looking back at that match will always trigger sad thoughts of the death of my father, just days before. What few are aware of is that it also symbolises the unforgivable harassment of my elderly mother in the most tragic of circumstances. Whilst all of that was going on, for my wife Beth and I there was turmoil in our lives that words can only begin to describe. Nobody but those closest to us knew that as I led my team out at Hampden, Beth was at home being cared for by doctors as we faced the terrifying fear that we could lose the baby we had waited twenty-one years for. Professionally it was the best of times, as a unique group of players achieved something that would have been unthinkable when I had first walked through the front door at Fir Park as manager seven years earlier. Personally it was the worst of times, as so many strands came together to bring an incredible strain on the entire family. There was a happy ending to 1991, though, with the birth of our little princess, Lorna. We had come through the tough times and were able to open a happy new chapter in our lives.

Looking back, it was the most intense period of my life and one that has helped me put everything else into perspective. There were tough times before then and great times too, just as there have been since. There's no doubt I'm a stronger person for all of those experiences.

It really began to build long before the Cup final on 18 May, when my Motherwell team was to line-up against my brother Jim and his Dundee United side. My mother had suffered kidney failure and my father was at the age where he was unwell, which in itself took its toll on my mum and her own health. Leading up to the match at Hampden, Dad was admitted to hospital. We had all been visiting as often as we could and knew he was fading, but that still didn't prepare me for the call on the Wednesday prior to the game to tell me to get to the ward as soon as I could. It is something you dread because you know in your heart of hearts what it means. By the time I arrived at the hospital, he had already passed away.

One of the particularly upsetting things was that the papers knew before I did. I believe one of the porters or orderlies had called the reporters before even the family had been notified – I can't begin to understand the thought process involved in picking up the phone in that way. It takes a certain type of person to do that. What they gained, I've no idea.

Jim was on his way through from Dundee, but I had to phone and tell him to take his time. It was too late. We obviously knew my father wasn't well – he was seventy-eight and not in good health – but nothing prepares you for it. My mother died just nine months after him. She never really got over his death.

Obviously my father's condition had been a huge worry for the whole family, but we clung on to the hope that things would change and he would be able to return home. Unfortunately, that wasn't the case.

It turned the whole period upside down for Jim and I. The prospect of the Cup final between our two teams had been a welcome distraction, but my father's death of course pushed our thoughts of Hampden far into the background. At the same time, we had a duty to our clubs, to the players and the supporters, but football was the last thing on our minds at that time. Bereavement is a shock to the system and we went through the process very much in the public eye, trying to put on a brave face.

There had been a suggestion in the media that the final could have been postponed, at least until after the funeral. Jim and I briefly discussed that, but neither of us felt it would have been the right thing to do. The day wasn't about us, it was about the tens of thousands of fans who had been building up to it for weeks and we didn't want to cause disruption to them. We also felt that Dad would have wanted us to go ahead. He would have loved to have watched it. Even if we had been of the opinion the game was too soon after his death, I don't think our thoughts would have held too much sway with the powers that be. Jim Farry was in charge at the SFA at that time and, being a stickler for what was laid down in black and white, he was adamant the final would go ahead on the date it was scheduled for. Our own timetable had been based around that date and we had to stick to that for the sake of the players.

I had planned to go away with my Motherwell squad on the Thursday, having booked what is now the Menzies Hotel in Irvine to take us away from the day-to-day hubbub surrounding the Cup final. We were fixed up to train at the Dam Park in Ayr on the Friday morning, the last session before the game, and everything was organised. After the death of my father my own plans went out of the window, but I had to keep things as normal as possible for those around me. I took the training on Thursday before the team headed away to Irvine, but decided against joining them down there. Instead I stayed close to home and travelled down the following day.

My brother Willie was a real rock for the family through that terrible time, a major force. As the eldest, he shouldered the responsibility for all of the arrangements and was a pillar of strength for everyone around him. For Beth and I it should have been a wonderful time in our lives, with our first child on the way. But with the stress of everything going on at home, Beth had a bleed. We were terrified we were going to lose the baby. We had waited twenty-one years and then all of a sudden there was that horrible feeling that we were going to have the most precious thing in the world taken from us.

Through our married life we had always wanted a little one to make our family complete, but it hadn't happened for us. We went through all of the tests and everything showed up fine, all the doctors could say was to wait and see. When Beth did eventually fall pregnant we were so, so happy – it was a sense of life becoming whole for us. The fear of a miscarriage is something every parent must go through at some stage during the pregnancy, no matter how fleeting that thought might be, but after waiting so long, it was a very anxious time for us both. When Beth had to call the doctor in the build-up to the Cup final, there was an aching sense of dread. There was little we or the doctors or nurses could do. Beth was ordered to rest in the hope that would be enough, with the doctor making house visits frequently to keep an eye on her. All we could do was hope for the best. It was still fairly early in the pregnancy, but by that stage our close family knew. That was the one comfort at the time of my father's death, that he at least was aware that the baby was due. He understood how important it was to Beth and I.

With everything happening at home, there was tremendous strain on us all. There's a tendency to try to keep things to yourself in times like that, to get through the other side, but really you have to confide in people and have to talk about it. I was able to do that because of the support around us.

All the time I was also trying to be fair to the players and to the fans. I didn't want to put a dampener on what was, naturally, a very big occasion. It was a once-in-a-lifetime event for many of those involved and they deserved the chance to enjoy every minute. I can't speak for the players, but I hope the events off the pitch were not allowed to impact on them. Of course, they were aware and I was touched by the respect and sympathy I received, but we tried our best not to let it dominate the days leading up to the game. The only difference they would have noticed was that I was not around as much as I perhaps would normally be, although I was adamant I still wanted the day-to-day involvement and to take on the work I would have done in the build-up to any other game. We went through the same routine of training, shaping the team and preparing physically as usual, and if anything that was a very valuable distraction for me.

It is amazing when you throw a bag of footballs over your shoulder and walk out onto the training pitch how, for a short period at least, everything fades to the back of your mind. It can be a therapeutic exercise, a little bit of escapism.

Although the shape of the team was done, I still needed to rely on my backroom staff of Tam Forsyth, Cammy Murray and the rest a great deal during that week. They kept things ticking over and my faith in them took away any of the stress or strain that there might otherwise have been. The players were great too. I trusted them implicitly to do what we asked of them and they did. I went down to the hotel in Irvine at 10pm on the Thursday night, ready to take training on the Friday morning. I dashed back up the road to be at home with the family later that morning, returning on the Friday night to be with the squad on the day of the match itself.

Wherever I was, I was constantly checking on Beth – that was a huge worry, even though we both knew there was nothing we could do. It was simply a case of waiting and hoping. I don't mind admitting that I wouldn't have cared whether we won or lost, as long as Beth and the baby were okay. Whilst, fortunately, we were able to keep the pregnancy and the scare surrounding the baby private, the death of my father was a big story for the press at the time. That was even more so because of the Cup final looming. Had it not been for that game I'm sure my father's death would have been noted, but it became headline news because of the timing – and not everyone covered themselves in glory at that time.

On the day of the game, Willie had been at home to spend a couple of hours with my mother. She was still terribly upset, understandably, and shaken badly by my father's death. Willie was on the staff at Motherwell at that time, working in the community coaching set-up, and left the house to make his way to Hampden for the match. Just after he had pulled away, a woman reporter turned up on my mother's doorstep. She must have been waiting for the chance to get Mum on her own.

My mother was an elderly lady, not in a position to handle that type of situation. She answered the door and was bombarded with questions – the main one being, 'Who do you think your husband would have wanted to win today, Tommy or Jim?' It was ridiculous, it was distasteful and it was a sad reflection on that particular newspaper. I wouldn't even give it the satisfaction of a name-check in this book, but those involved know exactly who they are. It wasn't one reporter acting on her own, she obviously had her orders to go out and try to get that story, but then she also had a conscience of her own, surely.

I was desperately disappointed with the way that was handled – there was no excuse. Jim and I were accessible enough to every paper in the land, so it would have been simple enough to make an approach through us. The answer would have been 'No', that it wasn't appropriate to speak to my mother. Which I imagine is why it was done in the way it was, sneakily and without an ounce of compassion for a wonderful lady who had just lost the husband she loved so dearly.

Willie had been in touch with my mum before the Cup final and knew what had happened. He took Jim and I aside to let us know, to avoid us finding out from anyone else, and at moments like that you do start to wonder what it is that you're wrapped up in. Again, we were both professional and knew we had to grin and bear it. We had ninety minutes of work to get through and we did that to the best of our ability. The history books show that it proved to be one of the most dramatic Scottish Cup finals ever to be played, Motherwell's 4–3 win is still talked about today. But whatever had happened in that game, we knew how the day would end.

Jim and I had made a pact that whoever won the game wouldn't be seen celebrating. Neither of us felt that would be appropriate in the circumstances and we were determined that, in our own private way, the match would be a fitting tribute to my father. The only public gesture we made was in leading out the teams wearing black ties as a mark of respect, everything else was kept between us in a dignified manner. That was the way it should have been and that was exactly the way it worked out.

I'm sure people must look back and wonder where I was on the day, because I only appeared in one or two photographs, even then it was reluctantly. It wasn't a time for me to be dancing around or spraying champagne. I think there's one image of me holding the cup alongside Stevie Kirk and Craig Paterson, when they had called me on to the track. Otherwise I tried to stay in the background as best I could, again without making it awkward for the players – I certainly didn't grudge them their time in the spotlight, they deserved to make the most of it and I hope each and every one of them savoured every second of that day. I'm certain they did. For me it was a time for reflection rather than celebration and in among the bedlam the quietest place to be was around our dressing room, with the squad still out on the pitch doing their lap of honour. Cammy Murray and Tam Forsyth came looking for me, but I sent them both back out. The chairman, John Chapman, came to congratulate me, along with his fellow directors Bill Dickie and Ian Alexander. It was a nice touch, but I told them to get back out and celebrate. They deserved the moment as much as anyone for the energy they put into the club.

Meanwhile, Jim found me sitting in silence in the little anteroom there was off the dressing room at Hampden. It was a very poignant moment. All we could do was fling our arms around each other. We had gone there knowing that one of us would win and one would be left disappointed, but there was far more to it than that. It had been a draining experience for us both and we felt for one another. As I say, the main thing was that we had produced a game that was a fitting testament to our father, a man who loved the game and who had instilled that passion for football in all of his boys. It was exactly the type of game that would have had him cheering and, just as importantly, it was played in the right spirit and in an atmosphere that was created by two great sets of supporters. He wanted us to make the most of our time in football and loved to talk about the game, loved the phone calls from his three boys to talk over this and that.

What we never lost sight of, no matter how tough a time it was for the McLean family as a whole, was that the Cup final made an awful lot of people very happy. For the Motherwell supporters it was an unforgettable time. We had won the cup and qualified for Europe for the first time.

The celebrations on the Saturday were not for me, but I put in an appearance out of a sense of duty and to show my appreciation to the players. The supporters had made their way to Fir Park and we went up into the directors' box to show off the cup, but I was there in body rather than spirit. My mind was a few miles down the road at home. The doctor had been back in to see Beth, who, it turns out, had been hopping in and out of bed in any case, switching the TV on and off as the Cup final unfolded. One minute she wanted to watch it, the next she couldn't bear the tension. By the Sunday the doctor was satisfied she would be able to get back on her feet and join me at Fir Park for the aftermath. It meant a lot to me to have her by my side, not least because I knew it signalled the worst was behind us in terms of the concern over the pregnancy. For Beth too it was important because after my father's death she was obviously worried about me, so we were a great support for each other.

Beth joined us for the open-top bus parade through the town and it was a real gala occasion. It made the work we had done building up the team and the club all worthwhile. I'd won plenty with Rangers but we were never allowed to parade the trophies, so it was a good experience from that point of view, putting a lid on what had been a memorable week for so many reasons, good and bad. My father's death, the Cup final itself, the parade through the town and then the funeral all came in less than seven days.

The time that followed was a very long and anxious six months but it passed without incident. On 6 November 1991, our little princess, Lorna, was born. For Beth and I it was our ultimate dream fulfilled, and that certainly puts your priorities in order. We had waited twenty-one years and after she arrived every moment was precious to us – Lorna was spoilt, there's no doubt about that. Quite rightly so. In football management you have to put in the hours, there's no nine to five and no paternity leave, but Beth was a star. She realised football was always going to be our livelihood and we were able to combine parenthood with work.

As every parent knows, those early years are tiring, but that's nothing compared to the joy Lorna had brought to our lives. She also almost brought me a few points on my licence when I was pulled over for speeding on my way from the ground to the hospital to see Beth and the new baby. Fortunately in the circumstances I was given a caution and told to be on my way. It was a hectic but joyful time, particularly after the pain we had all gone through at the time of my father's death, which remains the abiding memory of the earlier part of that eventful year.

I have to admit I've never watched the Cup final right through. I've seen highlights and the goals replayed at functions, but to sit down and go through the DVD minute by minute would bring back far too many raw emotions. Even after all this time, when I think back to that game I go through an incredible range of feelings. It takes you right back to the moment, and even after all these years, the pain is still there.

2

FOOTBALL IN THE BLOOD

Football is in my blood. I've heard plenty of people use that phrase in my time, but in the case of the McLean family, I think it might just be true. I've often been asked why I think my two brothers and I all made a name for ourselves in the game, and my honest opinion is that there is something in the genes. How else would you explain it? We were three boys from Lanarkshire who shared the dream of playing professional football with thousands of others. All three of us went on to live that dream and all three went on to manage at that top level. The odds on that would surely have been huge – but then again, we never really did predictable.

Willie, Jim and I perhaps didn't realise at the time, but what we had was unique. We were three different characters and led our own lives, but ultimately football was the common bond through some incredible adventures as players. That carried on into management, and when I look at the combined McLean roll of honour it is a source of great pride.

Willie, as the eldest, blazed the trail. As a player with Airdrie, Sheffield Wednesday, Alloa, Queen of the South, Clyde and Raith Rovers he served with distinction. As a manager with Queens, Motherwell, Raith, Ayr United and Morton he put all of his experience and knowledge to great use. Jim scored close to 200 senior goals as a forward with Hamilton Accies, Clyde, Dundee and Kilmarnock. Of course, it was as manager of Dundee United, over the course of twenty-two memorable years, that our Jim made his biggest mark and enjoyed his greatest success. Then along I came, the youngest son. I don't think there was ever much doubt about which path I would follow; the McLeans and football go hand in hand.

A quick glance at the family tree backs up my theory that there's more to it than just coincidence. My mother's father, William Yuille, was a forward with Rangers in the club's early years. He was in and around the team from 1908 to 1911 and scored a few goals by all accounts – so even before any of his grandchildren got their big break there was a player in the family. My father's side were no strangers to the beautiful game either, with his brother William playing for Third Lanark. My dad was a force to be reckoned with in his own right in the juniors. In fact, I'll never forget being told, 'You'll never be as good as your father' when I was starting to make waves as a youngster. Long after he had hung up his boots once and for all, people still spoke about him in glowing terms when it came to football – most considered him to be the 'top McLean'. The interesting thing is he actually gave up the game for the family, retiring early to concentrate on being a good husband, dad and businessman. He was a provisional signing with Hearts when he made the decision and was being talked about as a potential junior international.

We were brought up in the Plymouth Brethren, with the faith a big part of my mother Annie's family life. It was the commitment to the Brethren that led my dad to stop playing, something his father-in-law had encouraged. He threw himself into family life and building his bakery business and was a familiar sight on his van rounds in the area around the Lanarkshire village of Ashgill, where his three boys were born and raised. We were just a few miles from Larkhall, but it was very much a countryside upbringing for my brothers and me. I was the baby of the family, with Willie a full twelve years my senior and Jim ten.

As time went on the emphasis on the Brethren was more in the background and it certainly didn't impact on my life in a major way, although I think Willie and Jim had a greater involvement as youngsters. I went to Sunday school up to the age of around twelve, but it isn't something I have been actively involved with in my adult years. In saying that, even now Jim doesn't touch a drop of drink – something that has its roots in the church.

Had we had a strict church upbringing I don't think any of us would have gone on to play football, certainly not at the level we did, as the focus would have been elsewhere, just as it had to be for my father. Later in life I think he had a few regrets about stepping away from football early, although he would never say as much. The fact his three boys were so heavily involved in the game perhaps scratched that itch and he enjoyed coming along to watch each and every one of us. He wasn't short of an opinion or two either, a great source of advice.

My memories are of a happy and content childhood. Ashgill is a traditional mining village and although new houses have popped up here and there, it certainly hasn't changed beyond all recognition. Driving through now brings the memories flooding back. I went to Shawsburn Primary School and then Larkhall Academy, which is where I started to take football seriously. Up to that point I'd kicked a ball about and played the occasional game, but it was in secondary school that I got involved with eleven-a-side teams. By then my friends and I would be out playing until it got dark every night in rain, hail or shine. It was street football, park football . . . any type of football we could play, and right through until your mother roared out of the window for you to come back home.

It was during my time at the academy that two people in particular had a huge influence on what turned out to be the early days of a very long association with the game for me, Freddie Gibbons and George Hannah. Freddie and George took the school teams in those days, with Freddie responsible for the thirteen- and fourteen-year-olds and George taking the older squad. We had decent teams playing out of the school and it was when we had a game at the home park of Birkenshaw Amateurs, just a stone's throw from Ashgill, really, that the groundsman there decided to put together a side to play in the Under-18 league. Archie Hamilton was his name, the man who saw enough in a group of fifteen-year-olds to pitch us in against boys three years our senior. We should all thank him for that because it was a great education – you soon had to toughen up and learn the tricks of the trade. Speaking of tricks of the trade, I should say that Archie wasn't just a groundsman, he also worked with my father as a delivery driver. A small world indeed.

I was born on 2 June 1947, so by the time I started playing football seriously we were into the 1960s, and that decade was very much a golden era for the game in Scotland and for wingers in particular. Guys like Willie Henderson and Jimmy Johnstone were about to hit their stride and every team in the land had two wide men playing week in and week out. It would have been unthinkable to approach a match any other way. My dad, Speeder McLean as he was known, had been a right-winger too in his prime, so it was maybe mapped out for me to follow in his bootsteps. I was always small in stature too, so I had winger written all over me. It was the old McLean genes at work again.

The fact I grew up in and around football was a big influence on me. While I was starting out with the school team, Jim was plying his trade with Hamilton Accies and Willie was with Airdrie. To some people the thought of playing senior football was like a distant dream, but to me it was normal. I would go along to training with them and would be allowed to join in the five-a-side games at the end of the sessions. The routine would be for me to go along with Jim to Hamilton on a Tuesday night then with Willie to Airdrie on a Thursday. In hindsight, the two clubs were very good to me in that respect, as I was just a kid.

I can't overstate the way in which my two brothers shaped my career and, because of that, my life. I owe them a huge debt of gratitude for that, not least for the guidance they gave me in my formative years. Dad loved to come and watch us play, breaking away from his deliveries in the baker's van to take in the games when I was a teenager. When he couldn't make it along, Jim or Willie would be there for me.

Saturday nights in the McLean household invariably revolved around a seat by the fire or around the kitchen table for a debate on the good, bad or indifferent elements of the performance of yours truly earlier that day. Jim, Willie and my dad would go over it in fine detail, dissecting my game and helping me to improve. All three were very supportive and incredibly influential. The results were there for all to see: I didn't start playing eleven-a-side football until I was twelve, and by the age of seventeen I was in the Kilmarnock team to play against Real Madrid. It was a quick but very effective education. In many ways what I had growing up in the 1960s is exactly what we are trying to get back to in Scotland when it comes to rearing good young players. They have to be allowed to grow and develop, as I did playing in the street and in the park, without inhibitions but also need the experience of competitive football, as I did at Larkhall Academy, and the benefit of good advice from knowledgeable coaches, as I had at home.

It was while I was with Birkenshaw that the 'big teams' started to circle the wagons – word was obviously beginning to spread. Scouts began to approach, with a gentleman by the name of Angus McMillan at the forefront. He would be what you would class as a freelance scout, keeping clubs up-to-date with what was happening at grassroots level and presumably being looked after financially if one of his tip-offs came good. It was Kilmarnock who made the first move, sending out one of their own scouts after being given the nod by Angus and then inviting me down for a trial. We played Queen of the South in that game and won 7–2, a result I'm sure didn't do my cause any harm at all. I did enough to earn a second trial match, this time against Airdrie, and we won 3–2.

Willie Waddell was the Killie manager at that point, a wise old owl and with a real presence about him due to his status as a Rangers legend from his playing days. He made up his mind on the back of my two trial matches that he wanted me on the books at Rugby Park and travelled across to my parents' house to finalise the details – not bargaining on turning up to find another First Division manager at the house. That man was Mr James Scot Symon of the Rangers Football Club, so the two were far from strangers. It was as interesting an afternoon as I can remember for the McLeans at Ashgill.

It transpired that Symon had got wind of Kilmarnock's intention to sign me – they probably knew before I did, such was the nature of the game – and had dashed through to Lanarkshire to try and jump the queue. For a fifteen-year-old boy, it was quite a decision to make. On one hand was the opportunity to join an all-conquering Rangers set-up and on the other was the far less fashionable Kilmarnock, although, to be fair, the club was playing in Europe in the Fairs Cup by that stage. I chose Killie. The reason was quite simple: I wanted to play first-team football.

While I was confident in my own ability, it was made clear by Rangers that I would be recruited for the Ibrox third team and viewed as one for the future. With Kilmarnock, the intention was to go into the reserve side and push for a place in the first-team squad.

At that stage Rangers had Alex Scott playing in 'my' position, a hero to the supporters and incredibly talented player. Pushing him hard for the No.7 shirt was a young Willie Henderson, who, as a fellow Lanarkshire lad, needed no introduction. Willie's reputation in the area went before him; he was a star in the making. Faced with those two ahead of me in the pecking order, it would have been a pretty thankless task to push my way through. So I thanked Mr Symon for his offer, but told him I was unable to accept. The two men had been friends and teammates, but I'm sure Waddell enjoyed winning that particular battle. It wasn't often Killie got the better of Rangers in the transfer market.

I was confident I'd made the right choice and, in time, it proved to be absolutely the correct decision. My brothers and my father felt the same way about it – with the advice from Willie and Jim that if I was good enough then the big move would come in time. I actually took those words of wisdom with me to pass on when I moved into management in later life. I can remember in particular having that conversation with Gary McAllister and Tom Boyd when they were teenagers learning their trade at Motherwell. Both had their heads turned by clubs in England and I urged each of them to be patient and to choose wisely.

Perhaps the only one who had concerns was my mother, who quite rightly had one eye on my life outside of football. She was adamant I should get myself a trade, something solid to fall back on if the big dream turned out to be just that – fantasy. I think she had seen enough with Jim and Willie and those around them to appreciate that it takes more than talent to make it in professional sport. You need the right work ethic to go with it, but you also need a few decent helpings of luck along the way. That is the one ingredient you can't bring to the table yourself and it is particularly important early in your career, when you do the bulk of your learning. It was also an era in which full-time football wasn't a given, with Willie and Jim both part-time. Willie was a draughtsman, while Jim worked as a joiner with Wilson of Stonehouse.

Football was my only goal in life, but my mother was very pragmatic. With that in mind, I started working with the electricity board to give myself a foundation. I was part-time with Kilmarnock to tie in with my work and would train in the evenings, finishing my day job at 4pm and travelling through to Kilmarnock for training at 6pm. It was a journey of one hour and twenty minutes each way by bus, starting from Hamilton and going cross-country on the Kilmarnock and Ayr route. It wasn't glamorous or lucrative, but I loved it. Even though Rangers had been knocking on the door, quite literally, money hadn't been a factor in my career at that early stage so I was still an amateur when I joined Killie. I got my expenses for travelling, but that was it.

I did turn quite rapidly from amateur to junior while starting out at Rugby Park, although that was just a technicality. The senior sides liked you to register with a junior club because if you didn't, it was a long and drawn-out process to be accepted back by the juniors if you needed to make that step back. The record books show that I joined Kilmarnock from Larkhall Thistle juniors, but I never kicked a ball for them. My progress was pretty rapid and I was only part-time for around three months before I was called up to join the first-team squad full-time, joining some great professionals in the likes of Willie Toner and Frank Beattie, two gems who helped me learn my trade. They would all look after the youngsters and were very, very good to us. Then there was Billy Dickson, who I travelled through with, and latterly Ross Mathie, Jim McSherry, Jimmy Cook and the late John Gilmour, who made up the group better known as the Lanarkshire Squad. An experienced campaigner by the name of Jim McLean was also part of that crew for a season, with my big brother lending his experience to the Kilmarnock team.

It was harum-scarum stuff when we got together, with plenty of hi-jinks. I can still remember vividly standing in the foyer at Rugby Park as Jim McSherry's car, an old Wolesley, came rolling through the door after the handbrake had been let off. Just another day at training – we knew how to have fun but also when to knuckle down and do the hard graft.

The pranks were all part of growing up, and I really did go from boy to man while I was with the club. I joined as a fifteen-year-old and spent eight years at Rugby Park, so it was as a person as well as a player that I matured.

3

HITTING THE HEIGHTS

In the space of four years I went from playing my first competitive football as a schoolboy to taking on Real Madrid at the Bernabeu. To say it was a rapid rise would be a massive understatement. When you're young you don't tend to over-think the situations you find yourself in. I was living in the moment and enjoying everything that came my way, not least the huge games I was lucky enough to be involved with during what proved to be some of the greatest years Kilmarnock have ever had.

As it is so often said, hindsight is a wonderful thing. Back then we knew what was happening was different and was special, but we didn't realise just quite how important that chapter would be in the club's history books. Will Killie ever win the top division again? Will Rugby Park ever play host to the biggest names in world football? Both of those look unlikely, making our own experiences in the 1960s all the more notable.

I was just fifteen and a half when I made my debut for the first team, turning out against Hibs in the old Summer Cup at the end of the 1963/64 season. The tournament had been brought back to help clubs meet running costs with extra gate receipts, although neither of the Old Firm teams were impressed by the idea and sat out the competition. I made my entrance at the semi-final stage, although it wasn't the happiest of outcomes. We lost 3–0 at Easter Road to go out 6–4 on aggregate over two legs, with Hibs going on to win the cup after beating Aberdeen in a final replay.

And still the familiar McLean analysis continued. When my father couldn't make it through he would send my uncle Bill along to the Killie games to report back on my progress, obviously trusting his judgement given his exploits with Third Lanark in his own playing days. To have that support network was priceless to me.

It was after that first game for the top team that I was encouraged to give up my job with the Electricity Board, freeing me up to step up my training and join the full-time staff. Not that it was an instant turnaround, though. After that first game I dropped out of the first team and back into the wilderness and was told I had to keep working hard to push myself forward.

Off the pitch there was still an initiation process to go through though as well, with the senior players in the routine of going into the howf at the ground for a cup of tea before training and picking their horses for the day's races, and the likes of me being chased out for being no more than a kid. They were good at keeping your feet on the ground and making sure you couldn't get too big for your boots. Looking back, it would have been quite easy to get carried away as there were some incredible things going on at Kilmarnock at that time – we had success and we also had some huge games.

The 1964/65 season was my first full campaign with the first team, and what a year it proved to be. For me, it really began when I was pulled into the team for the Fairs Cup tie against Eintracht Frankfurt at Rugby Park. We had lost the first leg 3–0 in Germany and Hugh Brown had suffered an injury, so it opened up an opportunity for me to get some more experience in what most people – maybe even the manager – saw as a lost cause of a tie. He had come in for some criticism after the first-leg defeat and although he would never have admitted it in the dressing room, I doubt in his wildest dreams he thought we could turn it around. I was just a pup, still only sixteen, and wasn't fazed by the prospect of playing in Europe. It was the club's first adventure in the Fairs Cup and even though it looked a forlorn hope of progressing, there was still a full house at Rugby Park for the return match. The atmosphere was phenomenal, like nothing I'd encountered before. It may have been a wild and wet September night, but it was red hot inside the ground.

But Eintracht didn't appear to be intimidated, and it went from bad to worse for us when Huberts scored after just a couple of minutes, putting us 4–0 down on aggregate and at the start of what looked likely to be a very long evening. Then it started to happen – everything clicked for us. After a quarter of an hour we were 2–1 up through goals from Ronnie Hamilton and Brian McIlroy. Into the second half Jim McFadzean made it 3–1 on the night and 4–3 on aggregate. Suddenly mission impossible looked as though it might just be achievable. Jackie McInally levelled the tie at 4–4 in the eighty-second minute.

I was rubbing my hands at that point, looking forward to a replay on neutral territory and a foreign trip, as was the rule at that stage. Just as I was preparing to look out my passport and dust down the suitcase, Ronnie Hamilton went and ruined it by popping up in the dying seconds with the goal to make it 5–1 on the night and 5–4 over two legs. All joking aside, it was an astonishing comeback and arguably one of the finest European results ever recorded by a Scottish side.

It was perhaps the most unbelievable ninety minutes I have ever been involved in, and for a rookie like me, it was very difficult to take in. To this day, no Scottish team has ever again overcome a deficit of three goals in a European tie, let alone four. Police had to escort us off the pitch as hordes of Killie supporters celebrated on the park at full-time, and I can remember being carried shoulder-high in among the crowds. Being the baby of the team I got all the glory and, I have to say, I revelled in it.

It was just the most crazy night, an amazing result against a German team which had been in the European Cup final just a few years earlier. To this day the Kilmarnock supporters still talk about that result and performance. The official attendance was just short of 15,000, but I must have spoken to at least double that number who claim to have been there! It is another one of those great occasions that football throws up, the type you don't really realise what you have been involved in until the years roll past and you reflect on how steeply the odds were stacked against you. Mind you, we were brought back down to earth with a bump when we lost 6–1 to Everton over two legs. You can't win them all and what had happened against the Germans was a classic case of a huge effort in a one-off tie to pull off what most would have classed as mission impossible. We hit top gear that night and they just didn't have an answer. If they didn't know what Scottish football was all about beforehand, they certainly did by the time they boarded the plane to go home. It was like a whirlwind.

The funny thing was I had absolutely no inkling at all that I would be involved in the game, let alone any thought that we would turn it around. All of the players would report at 6.30pm for midweek games, waiting for Willie Waddell to come in and read out the team. He did his usual run through from one to eleven and when it came to No.7 it was 'McLean'. I think the rest of the lads in the room were as surprised as I was, but there was no time to think or to get nervous. That, I would imagine, was the logic behind the decision not to give me any warning – just as Waddell did many years later when he pitched Derek Johnstone in against Celtic in the 1970/71 League Cup final to such wonderful effect. Derek would say the same thing, I'm sure, that the adrenalin rush you get from a surprise like that in the build-up to a game gives you an extra yard of pace and an extra foot or two in your leap. Certainly it worked for me and it worked for DJ.

Waddell was great for me. He was the type of man who would encourage you if you were doing well and soon let you know if you weren't, although I do think he had a different relationship with different people. Given he had taken me on straight from school, I always thought he felt he had a father figure-type role to play in my career. That wasn't the case for everyone. At Rugby Park he would often have a real go at Davie Sneddon, no holds barred. That was mainly because he knew Davie would bite back and he'd get a reaction. What you soon discovered was that Waddell quite enjoyed conflict, perhaps because he usually came out on top. For some players I'm sure he figured that they played better when they had a bit of fire in their belly and he was always on hand to stoke things up when required. The bottom line is that Waddell knew about being a good manager and promoting good habits that stood me in good stead for the rest of my life.

He also knew how to take care of young players. After savouring the win against Eintracht Frankfurt, I was promptly whipped back out of the first team and given time to breathe. I didn't appreciate it at the time, but I do now. It was around the turn of the year midway through the 1964/65 season that I was re-introduced to a first team that was going great guns in the old First Division, the top flight. When the bells rang in '65, we were sitting just off the top of the table, with Hearts leading the way. It had been nip and tuck between the two clubs up to that point and as the New Year began we moved back to the top of the table as the run-in loomed.

It was far from plain sailing all the way and as the weeks rolled on, the lead continued to fluctuate, with our own mixed form taking us down as low as fourth in the final quarter of the season. We went five games without a win at one stage and the promise from early in the season was fading fast. But there was a lot of character in that Killie team and when the going got tough the tough got going. We went on an incredible run leading up to the final match of the season – winning six of our seven games and drawing the other. That point was dropped against Rangers at Ibrox, so it was a very decent return.

The late burst took us to within two points of the league's lead, with Hearts in pole position going into the final match of what had been an incredible campaign. And who was that final match against? Hearts. It couldn't have been scripted any better. We travelled across to Tynecastle on 24 April 1965 knowing that we had to win and win by two goals and not concede. At that time it was the goal average rather than simpler goal difference or goals scored that was used to separate teams tied on points, but the equation was clear enough before we kicked-off.

Tynecastle now is revered as one of the great football stadiums in terms of atmosphere. In the 1960s it was very different – in my mind, even better. The supporters were still right on top of you, just as they are now, but then with the terraces and the fans standing it felt as though the whole ground swayed in the direction the play was flowing. There were 37,000 packed in and, with the bulk coming from Edinburgh, most were expecting a home win. We didn't, and Willie Waddell certainly didn't. The manager approached the game as he had every other that season, he was a stickler for high standards and wouldn't settle for anything less. That day we lived up to his expectations.

My memories are still crystal clear, not least of the opening goal. I collected the ball out on the right wing and looked up to see Davie Sneddon running in at the far post. I whipped in the cross and Davie rose to meet it perfectly; Jim Cruickshank in the Hearts goal had no chance. It felt at the time like it happened in slow motion, all eyes on the Killie side fixed on that ball as it hit the back of the net. The adrenalin rush when it crossed the line was incredible, our chests were puffed out and the sense of belief grew. When Brian McIlroy hammered home a brilliant shot just a couple of minutes later, the confidence soared even further. We had to hold out for the second half and Hearts threw everything but the kitchen sink at us over the course of those forty-five minutes, but we were a well-organised team and had a bit of luck into the bargain to keep the home team at bay. There was also a truly wonderful save from our goalkeeper Bobby Ferguson in the closing stages, a moment that was just as important as the two goals we scored that day.

I had my own shot at glory after the break, when Brian McIlory teed me up inside the box, but Jim Cruickshank was sharp off his line and got down well to get a hand to my shot. That would have been the cherry on top of the icing on the cake, as far as I was concerned: getting my hands on a championship winner's medal in my first season as a professional was good enough for me. It was the stuff dreams were made of.

The sight of Willie Waddell leaping for joy at the sound of the final whistle will always live with me. I was just a boy, the magnitude of what we achieved at Tynecastle took years to sink in, but the manager must have known exactly what he had witnessed: it was a one-off. The celebrations carried on in the dressing room, but even in the depths of the stand we could hear the Kilmarnock supporters singing and chanting. They were not for leaving, not yet at least. The manager ushered us back down the tunnel to take another bow and we circled the pitch for a lap of honour, trying to soak up the moment. Up to that point the supporters had known nothing but near misses. Runners-up in the league four times, in the League Cup twice and once in the Scottish Cup ... Killie were always the bridesmaid. We had changed that and I'm still immensely proud to have been part of that magical season.

What made that season all the more incredible was the fact we had known as early as October 1964 that the manager was leaving at the end of the season. He had made his decision and announced his resignation. That could go one of two ways, either serving as motivation for the squad or bursting the bubble. In truth, I don't think there was ever any danger we would have gone flat – Waddell wouldn't have allowed it, not on his watch. He may have been serving his notice but not for a second did he let up, and he got his reward on the last day of the season.

When the announcement had been made in October it was a huge shock, both to everyone connected with Kilmarnock and to Scottish football as a whole. No real reason was given, no proper explanation as to what the manager had planned next. That led to a huge amount of speculation, with the reports at the time indicating he was being lined up as manager of the Scotland team. The SFA didn't exactly knock that out of the park, insisting they had not held talks with Waddell . . . but making it clear they would be quite willing to. On the back of what he had done at Killie, challenging for the championship on a shoestring, his reputation as a coach was strong. The man himself kept his cards close to his chest, save for making it clear that there was no problem in the relationship between him and the Rugby Park board. In fact, the directors were keen on adding their departing manager to their ranks in an attempt to retain his experience and expertise.

All of that talk and speculation could have been a distraction, but in all honesty players have an uncanny ability of being able to distance themselves from what is happening in the boardroom or manager's office. We were content to let those things take their course and concentrate on the job in hand, an approach which took us all the way to the championship.

Looking back, the aftermath of the title win was more than a little understated. After the champagne flowed in the dressing room, it was a case of finding our way home. I'd travelled by car to the match, so drove back to Kilmarnock for a small reception back at the ground. I don't think anyone had prepared for us winning and everything was spontaneous. The knock-on effect of winning the league was entry to the European Cup . . . and *those* games against Real Madrid. When we drew 2–2 at Rugby Park it was like winning the league all over again – they were full of world-famous names and had come to Ayrshire to be shown that all the talent on the planet sometimes isn't enough to get the better of good old-fashioned Scottish heart. Puskas was my boyhood hero and to get the chance to play against him was incredible. To score a goal in the same match capped it all, with a penalty giving me my big moment. When I scored that, the goalkeeper Antonio Betancort got a hand to it, with the ball just creeping in at the corner.

They did teach us a bit of a lesson in the return leg, beating us 5–1, but I would say the Bernabeu had a role to play in that. It was difficult not to be a touch overawed by the sheer scale of the place, although we didn't have much time to dwell on the surroundings, as they came at us in white wave after white wave over there. We were actually awarded another penalty kick and I was on duty again – this time the keeper was equal to it and saved it. I can still picture Betancort clutching the ball in one hand and wagging a finger at me with his other, as if to say,

'You're not getting away with that twice.' It was just another incredible instalment for me as a boy who had been thrown in at the deep end, and it was just the beginning of the adventure for me as a Kilmarnock player.

There were some incredible experiences along the way, ones that will live with me forever. There was the League Cup semi-final against Rangers in the 1965/66 season when I scored a hat-trick ... and still ended up on the losing side, with the other McLean, George, scoring a treble too as his side won 6–4. Our run to the semi-final of the Inter City Fairs Cup in 1967, when we ran the mighty Leeds United close, was another experience. Playing against the likes of Jack Charlton, Norman Hunter and Johnny Giles isn't something you ever forget! I sat out the first leg at Elland Road, when we lost 4–2 but was back in for the return at Rugby Park and we did our best to drag ourselves back into contention. With Leeds camped in to defend their lead, we struggled to break them down and had to settle for a 0–0 draw.

Then there was our tour of Rhodesia in the summer of 1970. Beth and I had only been married a few months when I was packed off to Africa with the rest of the Rugby Park squad to play a series of matches against local teams and select sides. There was none of the usual hotel luxury associated with foreign tours; instead we were each allocated a local family to live with, giving us a real flavour for the country and its people. We were treated fantastically by those who opened up their homes to us.

It was no normal tour, with the political situation in Rhodesia causing grave concern, after the white supremacist Ian Smith had taken power. The British government were opposed to the idea of sports teams going out there, but those in power at Kilmarnock were set on sending us, and when the SFA could find nothing in their rules to stop us travelling, it was given the green light. In hindsight I can understand the furore, but at the time, I have to admit, the players were not fully aware of the storm brewing. We went out to play football and were treated wonderfully by everyone we met, black and white, and I hope we made just as good an impression.

All of those events and many, many more mark out my time with the club, although winning the championship will always stand out as the highlight. It was a very special year, one in which everything came together at the right time.

For the players who had a hand in that run, the bond will always be there. We all went our separate ways in the years ahead but have been back together from time to time, including the fortieth anniversary in 2005. With the fiftieth just around the corner, I'm sure there will be many more opportunities to celebrate the good times.

4

LONDON CALLING

The Kings Road and Carnaby Street were iconic 1960s landmarks, the place to be seen for a generation in London. The question I had to answer was whether the bright lights were for me. The decision came in August 1967. I was twenty years old and approaching something of a crossroads in my career. I had gone from rookie to established first-team player at Rugby Park, even though my pay packet didn't particularly reflect that elevation. Killie were never going to be big spenders, run prudently and with one eye firmly on the balance sheet. I'd never criticise any club for that. There was a balancing act though, and as a young man making his way in the world I had to look out for myself. I was hedging my bets at that stage, holding out for a better deal at Kilmarnock and out of contract going into the 1967/68 season.

Long before the days of the Bosman Ruling, simply declining a new deal wasn't enough to make you a free agent – the club still held all the cards. They could still demand a fee and, ultimately, my future lay in their hands. Under the old rules, the only duty a club had to fulfil to a player to keep hold of them was to offer at least the same terms again. If, like me, you had joined as a boy and had only been with the one club, it meant there was no pressure on them to increase your pay as time went on. In fact, it was in the interest of the clubs to keep pay packets as slim as they could, as it made it far easier for them when it came to renewing the deals. Unlike the post-Bosman era, players had far less scope to move around. All I could do was try to force the issue and at least turn things to my advantage and by digging my heels in a bit I thought I'd at least get a little bit extra bolted on to my new contract.

The truth of the matter is that I was far from desperate to leave. I was a young man still learning my trade and had been well schooled at Rugby Park. In any case, with a league winner's medal tucked away, I had something that all the wages in the world couldn't have bought me. But I decided to keep my options open, not realising that I was obviously causing a little bit of concern in the boardroom. Behind the scenes the cogs were whirring, but the first I knew of that was when I was called into the manager's office.

Malky McDonald was the man in charge, having succeeded Willie Waddell, and in my mind I was going in to settle the contract issue – what I hadn't expected was the news that I could be on my way out. While my relationship with Waddell had been strong, I didn't have the same bond with Malky. It was Waddell who had given me my big break and I'd forever be in his debt for that, whilst the new manager, I felt, was cooler towards me. Malky was in his second spell in charge, having previously been manager in the 1950s, and had also been a player at Killie. He had the club at heart, but struggled to recreate what his predecessor had built.

When I sat down at his desk, I was told the club had accepted an £80,000 offer from an English club. That club was Chelsea, managed by none other than Tommy Docherty. He still kept a keen eye on the Scottish club scene, as so many of the teams south of the border did, and had been tempted to dig deep with what was a very decent bid. I didn't need any introduction to what my suitors were all about; everyone knew the Chelsea team of that era. With Charlie Cooke, Peter Osgood, Alan Hudson and others of that ilk in the side, there was no doubting their ambition.

They had won the League Cup south of the border in the same year we had won the First Division, and had come close to winning a Treble that season. The Doc had put his faith in a lot of young players, with the likes of Terry Venables and Bobby Tambling coming to the fore. In keeping with everything he did, Tommy was making waves at Stamford Bridge in what was his first managerial appointment. He was still well connected back home and had obviously been keeping an eye on my own progress.

By that stage in my career I'd been capped at Under-23 level by Scotland and played for the Scottish League select, as well as being called up for the senior Scotland squad that year. I fitted the mould of the type of young and ambitious player they were looking for at Chelsea. It turned out Tommy had already flown north to tie things up. He had been through to the club to agree the fee and then travelled to my house with Malky, aiming to get my signature before returning to London. I'm guessing neither of them expected for a minute that I wouldn't sign. It was a big move, to an exciting city and with the type of earning potential I couldn't even dream of at Killie. Or so I'm told. As it happened, I never got as far as talking figures when it came to wages. The Doc did say I'd be looked after and the papers were talking of an impressive £100 per week wage and four-year contract, but that wasn't my only motivation at that stage of my life or my career.

He was a powerful individual and not short of a persuasive word or two, he couldn't have sold the club or the league to me any better than he had done. But even as a young boy I could be single-minded – maybe it was another one of the McLean traits coming to the fore. It was one that served me well in what could have been an intimidating situation.

Chelsea wanted me to sign and Kilmarnock had 80,000 reasons to move me on. For the club it was a chance to pull in a record transfer fee – bettering the £65,000 they had raked in when Bobby Ferguson had been sold to West Ham just a few months earlier. For a club that had only gone full-time under Waddell's reign, they were figures that previously had been unheard of. I believe that transfer made Bobby the world's most expensive goalkeeper, but it wasn't always a bed of roses for him at Upton Park, with a lot of attention on him because of that price tag around his neck. West Ham conceded eighteen goals in a six-game spell early in Bobby's time there and he ended up being dropped, although he came back fighting and went on to show why they had invested so heavily, playing more than 250 games right through to 1980.

What Bobby's transfer had done was put Kilmarnock back in the black. In the 1965/66 season the club had posted a not insignificant loss of £21,000. On the back of the fee pulled in from West Ham, at the end of the 1966/67 campaign the annual accounts showed a profit of almost £37,000 and there had also been money invested in ground improvements. That was how important it was to Killie to produce players who could be sold on; it effectively allowed the club to stay afloat. We knew that as players, the supporters knew that and the directors never hid the fact. The interesting thing was that Malky MacDonald was not only manager but doubled as secretary at that time, so balancing the books was as much a part of his job as putting a winning team on the park. It was his name against the financial report each year, so there was extra pressure on him in that respect.

If Chelsea were willing to sign a cheque for £80,000 it would have eased the financial headache for a good few seasons. But the bottom line was that the decision was mine. I hadn't even been to London at that stage, but somehow it just didn't sit right with me. I was engaged to my future wife Beth by then and ready to set up home near to our own families in Lanarkshire, so it would have been a huge upheaval to start our life somewhere completely new to both of us. Neither of us had a burning desire to move away, and being a country boy at heart, the big city made we wary. My grandfather had bought land in Ashgill, taking over a mining row with a view to creating sites for houses, and had set aside plots for my mother, my brothers and I. By that stage, Beth and I were in the process of drawing up plans for our first house and applying for planning permission. It was an exciting time for us, a perfect start to our life together, and not something we were willing to turn our back on.

There were sound football reasons for not jumping at the Chelsea offer too. They were a glamorous club with some big name players – characters like Charlie Cooke and Peter Osgood – and, if the truth be told, I wasn't convinced I would be able to go into a dressing room full of high-profile players and make a big impression. I was never the most confident of boys, particularly at that stage in my career, and mixing with guys who were superstars in England worried me. As you get older that sort of thing worries you less and less, but at that stage it just wasn't the right fit for me. In the background the rumours about Rangers being interested in me continued to flutter around, undoubtedly another factor in my decision to bide my time.

Maybe some would look at the money and the profile of being centre stage with a big London club as being worth taking a gamble on regardless of circumstances or your gut feeling, but that is a dangerous route to go down. Unfortunately, particularly in recent years, too many good young Scottish players have jumped too quickly when there has been the prospect of a move south. I appreciate now the financial advantages are even greater than ever before, but there has to be a long-term view taken by players and their advisors. For English clubs now the investment to bring a Scottish player down, in terms of fees and wages, is tiny in comparison to the funds swilling around the game. Because of that they can afford to take a gamble on a young player, even if they've only played half a season in the SPL, and let them sink or swim. There's certainly no financial onus on the club to make it work because of the modest sums involved. For every one who has gone down and made a real go of it in England, a Gary McAllister or a Steven Fletcher, there have been another five or six who have faded into the background. You look at the likes of Kris Boyd, who was a hero at Rangers but toiled at Middlesbrough, and realise the road to England isn't necessarily paved with gold.

For some it is simply a case of too much too young, on and off the park. They go down and find they may be decent in the Scottish game but the standard in the wider world is far higher. That wasn't my major concern, as I felt I could cut it at that level, but it was more an inkling that if I waited there would be bigger and better things around the corner. That meant the man pulling the strings in the background would have to go back to the drawing board . . . with the power of the press driving the whole transfer, and in particular, the power of Jim Rodger.

Wee Jim, the renowned football writer, was perhaps the best-connected man in the game. He used to joke that if you needed a number for the Queen he could get it for you. In fact, it probably wasn't a joke at all, as his reach stretched the length and breadth of Britain and beyond. He classed Prime Ministers among his friends, not just his contacts. Long before the first agent had appeared in the British game, Jim was greasing the wheels and keeping things moving by putting people in touch with each other and making sure the right information was reaching the right ears. In return, he had a supply of exclusives to keep him going.

Jim was a fantastic man, a font of knowledge and a big character in Scottish football. Through his work with the *Daily Express*, *Daily Record* and *Daily Mirror* he made an enormous number of friends within the game and his death in 1997 was the end of an era for sports writing. When Jim spoke, you listened – so when he had mentioned in dispatches that Tottenham Hotspur and Rangers were also waiting in the wings, it is safe to say he had that on good authority, so I took it as gospel that there would be other moves in the offing if I chose to bide my time. It is far easier to keep yourself in check when you're confident that the opportunity you're considering isn't a last chance. For me it was too soon to be making the move and I had made my mind up, despite the best efforts of two of my mentors to change it for me.

My brother Willie and Willie Waddell, who by that stage was working in newspapers with the *Daily Express*, were adamant I should have grabbed the Chelsea opportunity with both hands. Our Willie had had a stint in England with Sheffield Wednesday and felt it was an arena in which I could thrive. It had been a short stop for him at Hillsborough, in between his time with Airdrie and his move to Alloa in 1960, but he had seen enough to be sure that the game south of the border was a good fit for me. Willie Waddell had phoned me at the house to tell me not to be too rash. He said I'd be made for life. Waddell told me he was away to jump in his car and would be at the house within half an hour, presumably thinking he'd be able to talk me round. It was still a bit of a teacher-pupil relationship between the pair of us – I was worried I was about to get the belt! Then he called to say he wasn't coming. He said he knew there was no point, as I'd already made up my mind. I heard the words 'foolish, foolish boy' being uttered before he rung off.

Even if he had come round and applied a bit of pressure, I wasn't for turning. The honest truth is that I had my mind made up within minutes of being told of Chelsea's interest. I simply gave them the courtesy of listening to what they had to say. It would have been a long trip for Tommy Docherty to make without even getting the chance to talk to me. In time, Mr Waddell had every reason to be glad that I had stuck to my guns. But more on that later.

The dalliance with Chelsea proved to be the end of Tommy McLean and English football, save for a few expressions of interest that never came to anything more substantial. Wolves were the club who were most active, both during my playing days and later in management, but it wasn't something I encouraged on either occasion. Whilst they were undoubtedly a huge club with great potential, it was another case of one that just didn't sit right with me either as a player or as a manager when the talk arose in two very different eras.

As a player I was with Rangers when the Wolves interest cropped up, so any move away would have been a huge step down. As a manager I was with Motherwell and building for the long-term. To give that up at that stage would have been very difficult. When it comes to managerial opportunities you of course have one eye on the potential of a club – and Wolves was and still is a club with great potential – but also at the prospects of exploiting that to the full. At that moment in time there just weren't likely to be the funds available to make a dent on a very competitive English league scene. Even then, money was king.

In the end, as a player I spent eight years with Kilmarnock and ten years with Rangers. I showed loyalty to those two clubs and wasn't interested in hopping around chasing a bigger pay packet or a new experience. I wouldn't criticise people who did things differently – playing football is a relatively short career and you have to go with your gut instinct. If that takes you far and wide then all well and good, but if you can fulfil your ambitions without moving on I don't see any problem with that. Loyalty is a hugely undervalued commodity in football and sometimes it pays to play the long game. The trick is in making the right decision at the right time and nobody gets that right on every occasion, but in my own case, I'm quite content with the choices I made and the path those decisions took me down. Had I gone to Chelsea I would have missed out on some incredible experiences with Rangers, so not for a minute have I ever regretted the decision to reject that move to Stamford Bridge. Mind you, if Roman Abramovich were to pick up the phone tomorrow and call me, I might be tempted to listen to what he had to say!

5

NATIONAL SERVICE

Four league championships with two different clubs, the European Cup Winners' Cup, the Scottish Cup four times and the League Cup on three occasions. My playing record is a source of great pride to me, as are the six games I played for my country. To win more trophies than caps is unusual, and in the current climate, it is difficult to envisage any player enjoying that type of success with their club making only a handful of appearances for Scotland, especially when you consider I played at the top level from the age of sixteen right through to my mid-thirties.

Bitter, resentful, angry. Maybe I could be forgiven for being all of those things, but in actual fact I have always been quite philosophical about my time with Scotland. Of course, I would have loved to have played in every international game over that eighteen-year period, but I was not alone in having to accept opportunities would be few and far between. You only have to look at my old friend Alex MacDonald, who played for Scotland only once, to see how difficult it was during that period. Doddie was a phenomenal player for Rangers over a long period, part of so many winning teams at Ibrox, yet could take nothing for granted when it came to Scotland.

In fact, the team that won in Barcelona in 1972 is another case in point. Willie Mathieson didn't win a cap; Dave Smith was Scotland's Player of the Year that season and finished his career with just two to his name. Then there was Doddie, myself and Alfie Conn, who was another who won just a couple of caps, as well as Peter McCloy with four appearances, a whole host of players who could perhaps point to being in the right place at the wrong time as far as international football is concerned. Would a home-grown Scottish team winning a European trophy in the current climate be likely to form the backbone of the international team? I think it's a good bet that would be the case, but it was a different time and there were Scottish players in pretty much every leading team in Britain.

The interesting thing with my own career in the dark blue jersey was that all six of my caps were won as a Kilmarnock player, the complete opposite of the usual perception of somebody making the move from a provincial side to either one of the Old Firm. I'd also won caps for amateur Scotland shortly after joining Killie as a young boy, which was a tremendous honour for me on the back of representing Lanarkshire at district level. Every time I stepped up a level I got the same buzz from being selected, with winning a place in the full international team the ultimate reward.

It was Bobby Brown who introduced me to football at that level, giving me my debut in a friendly against Denmark in Copenhagen in the autumn of 1968. We won that game 1–0 and a few months later I made my first competitive appearance in Cyprus in a World Cup qualifier in December 1968. It was a memorable occasion for so many reasons – not least the torrential rain and thunderstorms we played in, with huge puddles all over the pitch from start to finish. It was as far removed from the sun-soaked image of the island as you can get. In fairness, the conditions didn't do us any harm, winning 5–0 at a canter, with all of those goals coming before the break. I lined up in a team with the likes of Billy Bremner, John Greig, Billy McNeill, Charlie Cooke, Ronnie McKinnon and Colin Stein. It's fair to say it was a very good generation to be picking from.

Throughout my time being involved in a number of squads, I was playing second fiddle to Willie Henderson and Jimmy Johnstone for a place in the starting eleven, which is no disgrace, considering the calibre of those two players. I've got a collection of Scotland jerseys and the bulk of them are No.15 or No.16 from those stints on the bench. With substitutes still rarely used, it restricted me to stepping in when there were openings and making the most of those games when I was on from the start.

The trip to Cyprus was one of those matches, a good introduction to the ups and downs of life with Scotland. I'll never forget looking over to the side of the pitch and seeing the press pack all lined up behind desks within touching distance – including Willie Waddell, right at the front. They were as sodden as the players, with not a scrap of cover anywhere in the ground. Bobby Murdoch scored a couple, Alan Gilzean got two as well and Colin Stein wrapped things up just a couple of minutes before half-time. What could have been a difficult ninety minutes turned out to be a walk in the park and I came through my first game with flying colours, getting some good reviews in the reports that followed. It was one of those games where just about everything I tried came off for me, a real pleasure to play in. I say just about everything – I came within inches of capping my debut with a goal, or two to be precise. The Cypriot keeper got down well to smother one of my shots early in the game and then again in the second half he produced a tremendous diving save. A goal would have been nice, but I went away happy with my day's work. In a tough qualifying group we were level with Germany on four points after that game in Cyprus.

I had to wait six months for my next outing in Scotland colours, this time in slightly more forgiving conditions at Wrexham as we took on Wales at the Racecourse Ground. To say it was eventful was an understatement, with goals flying in left, right and centre – not to mention a few casualties of the old home international rivalry. We were two goals ahead within the first sixteen minutes, with Billy McNeill and Colin Stein putting us in front, but Ron Davies and John Toshack scored to peg it back to 2–2. Then we lost our keeper at half-time, with poor old Tommy Lawrence in the wars. He took a bang in the face and broke his nose, so it was Jim Herriot who came out for the second half. Alan Gilzean put us in the lead again, but Davies levelled it at 3–3. It wasn't until the seventy-second minute that Billy Bremner put us back in front, and then I chipped in with what proved to be my one and only international goal to give us a 5–3 win. It was a nice way to round off an amazing game.

I took a knock to my ankle in that game, and although I was back on my feet by the time we went south to play England at Wembley in the next game, Bobby Brown chose to err on the side of caution and left me out. While the rest of the troops were heading for London, I was on a plane destined for America to join the rest of the Kilmarnock squad for a close-season tour in the US. If I have one regret in terms of Scotland, it is that I didn't make it for that match. Running out to play the Auld Enemy at Wembley is something every young boy dreams of, and I was no different. Unfortunately, it was always a case of so near yet so far for me – I made the bench on another occasion and the atmosphere was mind blowing. You couldn't hear yourself think, just bedlam. What I did prove to be during that period was a bit of a lucky omen. Every time I played, we tended to pick up a result.

My fourth cap was in 1970 against Northern Ireland at Windsor Park in Belfast and we came away with a 1–0 win, courtesy of

John O'Hare. There never seemed to be a dull moment with Scotland and that game was absolutely no different. It was a tousy affair, with lots of grappling and some meaty tackles flying in all over the pitch, so it was no surprise when there was a red card, although the circumstances were a bit odd.

It was George Best who was in the middle of it all, as usual. He'd missed a couple of decent chances and was starting to let frustration get the better of him, complaining to the referee that he was being fouled. When his claims for a free kick were waved away, Best bent down and picked up some clumps of mud and turf and hurled them at the referee. And that was that, Northern Ireland were down to ten men. We still had to make the extra man count and eventually we did that, with John rising perfectly to get his head on a ball I'd swung to the far post. It was a peach of a goal and turned out to be the winner.

Four days later, I had my first experience of playing for Scotland at Hampden, in a 0–0 draw against Wales, so could tick that off on the 'to do' list. If only football was as simple as that! The Welsh hadn't won at Hampden for eighteen years so we were favourites to win, but in the end a draw was a fair result. They had come for a draw and got that with a real backs-to-the-wall-type performance. Pat Stanton, who had just been named Player of the Year in Scotland, had to pull out the day before the game due to a bout of flu so there was a bit of a last-minute reshuffle during the final training session down at Largs.

We had a young team out that day, myself included, but we put on a decent show on another rainy international night. There was certainly an emphasis on pressing forward, but we couldn't break them down. There were more than 30,000 inside Hampden for that game and the home internationals were brilliant to be involved in, and even today I think there would be the same passion, something that can be lacking in the international fixtures. Not that I think we'll see them come back, the logistics are just too complicated, particularly when it comes to the prospect of regular Scotland v England matches. Aside from that, the club schedule is getting more and more congested and the windows for rest are shrinking all the time. Adding more games to the mix isn't really an option.

In time the attraction of the home internationals began to fade, with more and more withdrawals impacting on squads. I can understand club managers taking a selfish view on it, but it wasn't a road I would ever have considered when I was coaching. I viewed every match for Scotland as an honour when I played and as a manager I wouldn't have denied anyone the chance to go and represent their country, I viewed it as a reward for their efforts. I had the pleasure of informing quite a few players that they had been called up and it was one of the more enjoyable tasks in club management.

When you're playing the novelty never wears off, with every invite to join the Scotland squad as satisfying as the first. My sixth appearance, and what I didn't realise at the time would be my last cap, came during the tour in which I became a Rangers player. Although I had agreed to move to Ibrox while out in Scandinavia, when we played Denmark in Copenhagen on 9 June 1971 my registration hadn't yet gone through, so on the team list I was still 'Tommy McLean (Kilmarnock)'. It was the one and only game for Scotland that I came away on the losing side, going down 1–0. Ironically, it was arguably my best performance in an international and I came away with the Man of the Match award, sponsored by the Tuborg Brewery. They had just become part of the Carlsberg group and my reward was a pass to the brewery and the entitlement to drink as much of the product as I cared to. Being a good professional, I declined that kind offer! It was an interesting exercise from a Scottish point of view, with a number of fringe players involved against a very composed and patient Danish side. It was a sign of things to come, with the Scandinavian nations emerging as a force and leading the more established international teams, including ourselves, to up our game in the long-term to stay competitive.

I carried on with the squad to Russia during that tour but missed out on the game through injury, not featuring again in the years that followed but being in and around the squad. It was unheard of at that time to call off without a genuine reason or to retire early from international football and it wasn't something that even crossed my mind, even if it was draining to travel without getting the reward of a game at the other end of it. I looked on every game for Scotland as a bonus and wanted to be involved. I was always conscious that those being picked ahead of me were good players – guys like Willie Henderson, Jimmy Johnstone, Peter Lorimer and Willie Morgan. Of course you have confidence in your own ability and believe you could do just as good a job as anyone, but at the same time you have to respect those around you. Perhaps if I'd been sitting on the bench looking out and thinking whoever was in the No.7 jersey couldn't lace my boots then I would have felt differently, but I genuinely never had that sense. It was a rich period for Scottish football with a lot of talented players vying for jerseys in every area of the pitch, so to be involved was a privilege.

Bobby Brown is the man who pinned his faith in me, with all of my appearances for Scotland coming during his tenure. Bobby had first seen me at really close quarters during the national team's training get-togethers down at Largs. Walter McCrae, the Kilmarnock manager at the time, was on Bobby's coaching staff with the SFA and he would enlist four or five of the Rugby Park squad to make up the numbers for bounce games involving the Scotland squad. More often than not, I was one of those sent along the road and I can remember some really good battles with Eddie McCreadie, of Chelsea fame. Getting the better of Eddie in those games certainly didn't do my international chances any harm at all, and I think it was those low-key afternoons at Largs that helped push me up the list.

It is little breaks like that can go a long way in football, although by that stage I was playing more and more with Kilmarnock and had been involved in some huge games. I like to think I acquitted myself well in those matches, including the European ties, and proved that I could live in the best company.

It was exactly the same after I had moved to Rangers, with regular league wins and Cup finals, as well as huge continental ties. In my mind I continued to develop and improve as a player at Ibrox, but the Scotland managers who followed Bobby Brown went in a different direction. That was the job they were there to do. The main thing is I can look back on the games I played for Scotland and say I don't think I could have done any more. No regrets, just good memories.

6

BLUE IS THE COLOUR

Which Scottish player was transferred from one Scottish club to another Scottish club in a foreign country and played for a third team in one day? That's the trivia question that has followed me ever since I made my move to Ibrox. Kilmarnock, Scotland and Rangers within the space of just a few hours was how one of the most surreal days in my life panned out – made all the more odd given it was played out in the Scandinavian town of Vedbaek.

I was in Denmark as part of a Scotland tour during the summer of 1971 when the whirlwind was whipped up. We were based at the Marina Hotel and had been out for training on the eve of the game. It was a light session, a loosener after the flight across and the chance to work on shape and set pieces. I knew from the way that session had gone, with a lot of the work revolving around me and my deliveries, that there was a good chance I would be playing so I was in good spirits when we went back to the hotel for a bite to eat. The rest of the afternoon was free time, a chance to relax and rest up before the match.

It turned out to be anything but relaxing for me, with the manager, Bobby Brown, taking me aside to say a delegation had arrived to meet me. They turned out to be familiar faces. One was Willie Waddell, the recently appointed Rangers manager, and the other was his Kilmarnock counterpart, Walter McCrae, my boss. Given we were a few miles from home, I gathered they weren't popping in to wish me well for the rest of the trip and with the two of them together there was obviously something going on.

Before I'd flown out with the Scotland squad there had been a couple of approaches from Rangers which had been turned down flat by Killie, who were prepared to play hardball. The sticking point, as is usually the case, was money. Waddell was in the process of shaping his squad and it was pretty much a 'one in, one out' policy. With that in mind, he was aiming for player swaps wherever possible and had offered cash plus a player in exchange for me. But Kilmarnock weren't keen on the swap element; they wanted a straightforward fee. By the time the first offer was rejected, I was aware of what was going on behind the scenes and I would be lying if I said my head hadn't been turned by the interest from Ibrox. From my point of view, a move to Rangers ticked all of the boxes. When that first offer was rejected I wasn't convinced there would be a second bid. When that second approach was knocked back, I was even more fearful. But Waddell and McCrae were thick as thieves by the time they touched down in Denmark and had clearly cooked up a deal between the two clubs to get things rolling again. When Waddell had been manager he had McCrae on his coaching staff, so there was already a link between them.

They had taken over Room 226 at the hotel to set up camp for the talks. I was told that a fee had been agreed and was squirreled away by Waddell to open talks on the personal terms. He told me he'd love to be able to look after me, but said the fact he had been forced to pay a big fee meant he would have to leave it to Killie to take care of me when it came to providing the signing-on fee, or a loyalty bonus on the back of my eight years' service.

So then it was left to Walter McCrae and I to thrash out the details. He told me that since they had been forced to settle for such a low fee that there was no way they could pay me any slice of that sum to smooth my exit.

The two of them were playing me like a fiddle, but I knew exactly what was going on. We had been in talks most of the day when we took a break in the early evening. I took the opportunity to call my brothers for some guidance and advice, and both agreed that I was right not to give any ground. We went back in for another round of talks and I told Walter the deal was off, that I'd go to the press and tell them that Kilmarnock had put a spanner in the works. I got a nervous reaction from the manager. He tried to tell me I couldn't do that. He knew fine well that I could, and that I would. Eventually, after another three hours of talks and me yo-yoing in and out of the room as the other two got together to chew things over, everything was settled. There was an element of compromise on all sides, but we got there in the end.

Although the two of them had arrived at the hotel completely unannounced, the prospect of the transfer had been rumbling on since the turn of the year. Because of that I felt I was in the driving seat. Rangers were clearly keen, not least because of my relationship with Waddell from our time together at Kilmarnock. For their part, Killie were not in a position to dictate, as they knew that if I dug my heels in I held the key. Added to the equation was the fact both McCrae and Waddell had come all the way out to Denmark, which suggested they both wanted things wrapped up quickly.

The prospect of joining Rangers was huge for me. I had loved my time with Kilmarnock and had a wonderful football education, but the time was right to make the next move – on and off the park. Kilmarnock had made it clear they were moving towards part-time football, and for myself and the rest of the players, that represented a crossroads.

Beth and I had been married for a year by the time I switched to Ibrox and getting some security was important to me. I had been fortunate to be with Kilmarnock through a period of full-time football, but Rangers was a different proposition altogether. It was obviously a massive club and with that came the challenge and the rewards that went with it. Importantly for me, both of my brothers agreed Rangers was the perfect move for me at that stage in my career. The club had gone through a lean spell in terms of trophies and was in transition, with Waddell relatively new in the manager's job. He had started to make his mark on the squad in a way that was no surprise to me. His predecessor, Davie White, had brought Jim Baxter back to Ibrox, but he didn't fit the Waddell identikit. He wanted discipline, work-rate and ability in equal measure. Jim was coming to the end of his career and didn't tick the first two boxes so was out on his ear.

I had cost in the region of £70,000 and represented a sizeable investment at that time, so the manager had put his faith in me. When he spoke to the press after concluding the deal in Denmark, the big focus was on which position I had been bought to play, or, in other words, who I had been taken in to replace. That was where Waddell was quite clever, replying that I could play in any position and that my arrival would keep a whole host of his players on their toes. He spoke of me as being ready-made to play on either wing or anywhere across the midfield, but I don't think he ever really had any intention of playing me anywhere other than on the right wing. It wasn't until later in my career at Ibrox that I shifted inside and played more of a holding role on a regular basis. What the manager was trying to do was take a little bit of the pressure off me and keep a few people guessing.

Going in being lauded as Willie Henderson's replacement would have been daunting for any player because he was a unique talent.

My first game at Ibrox, the first chance to sample the experience of playing in front of 50,000 Rangers supporters as a home player, was in a friendly against Everton at Ibrox at the start of August and, as I predicted, it was on the right wing that I was posted. Willie Henderson was on the casualty list ahead of that game, struggling with an injured toe, so from that point of view, there was no explanation required when I ran out with the No.7 jersey on my back. The talk in the build-up to that game was of the expectation on me going into the season and I knew all eyes would be on me, not least if it was in place of Willie that I came in to the team.

To be perfectly honest, I wouldn't have cared where I was asked to play because Rangers was a dream move for me. As I said at the time in my first round of interviews, I was 'on top of the world'. Unfortunately my first few months at Ibrox were something of a nightmare. In many ways the cause and the cure lay at the hands on one man: Jock Wallace. There can't be a football supporter in the land who hasn't heard tales of Jock's fitness regime, the gruelling sessions on Murder Hill at the Gullane Sands and the military-style approach to physical training. It was brutal and it was relentless, like nothing else I'd ever experienced. I've no idea what the sports scientists would make of it, as the approach was far more industrial, but the results were not in doubt and it also doubled as a great way of team-building as we pulled each other through.

Many have credited Jock's incredible methods as the reason for their longevity, with players like Sandy Jardine seeming to get better with every year as they sailed on effortlessly as if they were ageless. Me? I almost had my Rangers career pulled from under me because of exactly the same approach from a man who went on to become a hugely positive influence on my career.

In the early days, however, Jock got it wrong with me. I came in at the start of the 1971/72 season and virtually from day one he had me in the gym lifting the same weights as giants of men like Colin Jackson and Peter McCloy. I'm sure it hadn't escaped his attention, but I was no giant! I started off weighing 9st 5lb and put on 7lb in muscle before I knew it. The net result was that I was slower, less mobile and basically top-heavy. I had put on bulk around my shoulders, chest and upper body so had changed physically in a very short space of time. My body shape had been altered and the way I moved had changed as a result, obviously impacting on my game.

After toiling for a little while, it got to the point where I had no choice but to sit down with Jock and tell him that his training was affecting me – all the time thinking he'd probably see me as a malingerer. Here was me, a wee lad from Lanarkshire just in the door, telling the Jungle Fighter, as Jock was known, that his training was too tough. I didn't fancy my chances of success and half expected to be given double sessions as punishment. He didn't suffer fools gladly and certainly had no time for those who tried to shirk the hard work. But my fears were unfounded. Very quickly Jock acknowledged that the training was not right for me and changed things around. Soon enough he had me lifting half what the bigger members of the squad were and doing shorter, sharper repetitions. The edge to my play that I had lost came back and before long I was flying.

It wasn't just on the physical side that Jock proved to be adept. He had the right approach mentally too. After an indifferent start to my life at Rangers, to put it nicely, he took me aside and told me to stop trying to please everyone. In a nutshell, he had got to the root of the problem. I was busting a gut trying to win over a set of supporters who had been spoilt with wingers like Alex Scott and Willie Henderson. I was busting a gut trying to prove myself to Willie Waddell and Jock Wallace. I was busting a gut trying to show my teammates why I'd been brought to Ibrox in the first place. What Jock said was quite right: by trying to be all things to all men I was being my own worst enemy. He told me to go out and play my own game, to remember that really the only people that mattered were himself and Willie Waddell.

He said, 'You have to realise that we sign players for what we see and because we like what we see. Go out and please me, not anyone else. Please me and you'll be in the team.'

I took that advice on board and from then on didn't look back, really starting to hit my stride and as the fitness levels began to settle down. Had it not been for Jock's intervention, who knows where I would have ended up, certainly I don't think I would have gone the distance at Ibrox. For any new Rangers player a good start is important. Losing 2–0 to Celtic at Ibrox in your first game doesn't really qualify as a good start, which is exactly where I began. It was in the old League Cup group sections and the luck of the draw had the two of us in the same pool. We won our games home and away against Ayr and Morton but lost 3–0 in the return against Celtic at Ibrox, meaning we didn't make it out of the group.

That was all before a game had been played in the league, so not an ideal way to build confidence ahead of the big kick-off. I was on a bit of a hiding to nothing, having come into the team in place of Willie Henderson, and the results against Celtic didn't help my cause. In all honesty, my performances in those early games were not up to the standards I set myself.

When the league fixtures opened up we started with a surprise 3–2 defeat away to Partick Thistle and were beaten by the same score by Celtic at Ibrox the week after. It was going from bad to worse, and from a personal point of view, it wasn't ideal when I dropped out of the team after that Celtic match and Willie Henderson came back in.

Willie was such a hero to the supporters and deservedly so, he was a legend. Trying to fill his boots was a tough ask, but in truth, although I was wearing 'his' No.7 shirt the job I was being asked to do was different. Willie was a tricky winger in the traditional mould, an out an out attacker, whereas I was more of a midfield player, tracking back as well as being given licence to get forward down the flank. It was a subtle change in emphasis by Willie Waddell, sacrificing the luxury of an out-and-out winger to make the midfield more of a compact unit without taking away the attacking options – just in a more direct fashion, with my game centred around passing, crossing and dead-ball delivery rather than long and winding runs with the ball at my feet.

The other reason I never viewed myself as Willie's replacement is that I've always believed the manager had it in mind that we could play in the same team together, borne out by the fact we had worked it that way during our pre-season trip to Scandinavia, with me on the right, Willie Henderson on the left and Willie Johnston playing through the middle. Had it not been for a foot injury Willie Henderson suffered before the competitive games started, I would imagine all three of us would have been in the team. As it happened, wee Willie dropped out of the side because of that problem and I was pushed out on the right in his place. To the supporters, it very much looked as though I was there in his place.

In time that was the way it proved to be, with Willie moving on and the shape of the team evolving to tie in with the manager's plans to adapt the way we played, something that came into its own during the European campaign that season. What he was trying to do was modernise and introduce a more continental style, borrowing from what the Italians and Germans were doing but combining that with Scottish passion and urgency. Fast and fluid passing football was what we were being encouraged to play, something I thrived on.

The system was overhauled to fit with the new approach. Overlapping full-backs in the shape of Willie Mathieson and Sandy Jardine were introduced, a sweeper in the shape of Dave Smith was utilised in another nod towards what was happening in the European game and there was a big and small combination up front with Willie Johnston given licence to push up and play off Colin Stein. They were all concepts that have stood the test of time.

As with any change in any line of work, there was a period of adjustment. The difference in football is that the process is played out in full public view, there's no hiding place. Having gone out of the League Cup at the group stage and fallen behind Celtic and Aberdeen in the championship, the big question among the supporters and the media alike was whether the Waddell way would necessarily bring rewards. He had obviously had his success with Kilmarnock, but Rangers was a different proposition. At Killie winning games week in and week out was a bonus, a fairy tale. At Ibrox winning games week in and week out was what was expected. That brings its own pressures and also makes experimentation all the more difficult – there's so little margin for error and every decision is analysed and chewed over again and again.

When results early in that campaign did not go our way, it had all the hallmarks of a long, hard and barren season for us. Then along came the European Cup Winners' Cup and everything changed.

7

THE BARCA BEARS

The European Cup Winners' Cup tie in Portugal against Sporting Lisbon during the run to Barcelona in 1971/72 has gone down in history as one of the most bizarre nights in Rangers history. One minute we were out of the competition, the next we were back in. The defeat on penalty kicks and rapid reinstatement by virtue of the away-goals rule made all the headlines on that occasion, quite rightly. It was an incredible sequence of events and we were a whisker away from missing out on a place in the next round that was rightfully ours.

The sickening injury suffered by Ronnie McKinnon that night was the other major talking point, a real blow that sadly he never fully recovered from. It was the beginning of the end of Ronnie's Ibrox career. With so much going on, quite rightly my own role in the game against Sporting barely merited a mention in the post-match analysis. But on a personal level, it proved to be a hugely significant moment.

Having missed the two previous European ties, I came back into the team as a late substitute for the injured Willie Johnston out in Portugal, and from that point on I kept my place as all the drama of that run unfolded. The build-up to that moment for me didn't start in the international departure lounge of an airport. Instead it was a few months earlier in the less glamorous surroundings of Brockville, before we were due to play Falkirk in a league match in September 1971.

The start we had made to the season was bad, losing three times to Celtic in the League Cup and First Division underlined that fact. For me, being new to life with Rangers, it was a shock to the system. I'd come from Kilmarnock, where we had two or three big games per season, to Ibrox where every game was like a Cup tie – win or bust. The enormity of it all hit me on the afternoon we arrived at Brockville to play Falkirk. It was in a relatively low-key game but it was also the day that I was dropped from a football team for the first time ever – and it hurt.

The manager came in and read out the team and my name wasn't in it. Then he disappeared, as usual, for ten minutes and I was left to sit and take in what had just happened. It doesn't matter if you're playing primary school football or at the very highest level, the feeling is just the same. It's a slap in the face and a hard dent to your ego. For eight years solid I'd been a professional player and week in, week out I was in that starting eleven. Being Willie Waddell, there was no conversation or no explanation. I was out, simple as that.

At that stage you either go in a huff or you roll the sleeves up – there's no doubt you look for someone else to blame, but ultimately I knew in my heart that it was the right decision. I hadn't been playing well and being dropped from the team was food for thought. I also think it sent out a message from the manager that I wasn't the teacher's pet, I'd be treated the same as everyone else whether I was a big signing or not and whether he'd had me under his wing as a kid or not.

I came back into the team after a couple of games but flitted in and out for a period, culminating in the return to action in Portugal against Sporting Lisbon. There can't be a football fan in Scotland who doesn't know what happened next, but in the interests of completeness, it is worth going over it all again. Leading 3–2 from the first leg in Glasgow, we lost 4–3 on the night in Lisbon to be tied at 6–6 on aggregate. We lost the penalty shoot-out, trudged off the pitch and were sitting in virtual silence when John Fairgrieve, one of the travelling journalists, appeared clutching the rule book and pointing to the fact we should have gone through on the new away goal rule. I'm not sure what the UEFA observer in the stand was doing when all of this was going on, but that's another matter altogether.

Suddenly the gloom lifted and when it was confirmed the referee had made a mistake, the sense of relief was incredible. We had a second chance and, when you've been out of the competition and suddenly find yourself back in, you start to think that maybe this is your year. Sporting Lisbon were a very good side with some top-class players and to have put up such a spirited fight was a huge confidence boost. I'm not a great fan of the away-goal rule by any stretch of the imagination, but on this occasion it was very welcome. What it has served to do in the years since we benefited from it is to stifle European ties, the first priority for home teams is not to concede that all important away goal. What you want is for the home team, with their own crowd behind them, to be free to attack and go at the visitors but the away-goal rule flies in the face of that.

In Lisbon, with neither team aware of the rule or at least sure of it, the goals were flying in. I think it was after that game that I started to play with the type of confidence I had done at Kilmarnock and I kept my place for the remaining European ties, right through to the final at the Nou Camp. As it happened, I was in at the start and in at the end of the run, missing out on two of the games in between. When we went out to France to play Rennes in the first leg of the first round I was the man in possession of the No.7 jersey, with Willie Henderson left kicking his heels.

We came away with a 1–1 draw, courtesy of Willie Johnston's goal, but by the time we beat them 1–0 at Ibrox, it was my turn to sit on the sidelines. It was the same for the 2–2 draw with Sporting Lisbon at home in the first leg of the second round and for the trip to Portugal for the return match I was still out of the starting eleven. The Lisbon tie proved to be the turning point for me in that run. Substitutions were still rare back then. The manager needed both of his subs that night.

Dave Smith, coming back after a broken leg, was introduced to replace the stricken Ronnie McKinnon after his horrendous injury. I got my chance when Willie Johnston came off through injury, so we finished off the match with both Willie Henderson and myself in the same team – me on the left and him on the right. I got on well with Willie – I still do – and always thought we could have played in the same team on a regular basis. Willie Johnston enjoyed playing through the middle, so there was certainly room for all three of us. But Willie Waddell was beginning to think otherwise and it was as much to do with the type of personality he wanted in his side as anything else.

After the result in Lisbon, we came back and thumped St Johnstone up in Perth, winning 4–1 in the league, but there was a long hiatus in Europe. We played Sporting on 3 November 1971 and didn't play the quarter-final against Torino until 8 March. It was up to the manager to keep the focus on Europe without letting us take our eye off the ball in the league.

It was a new team in the making and the delay may not have been the worst thing for us. It gave us four months longer to gel and to work together, four months to prepare ourselves for two of the biggest games in the history of the club. Torino were a considerable obstacle. After the flair of the Portuguese, it was very much a case of the steel of the Italians.

On the eve of our first leg in Turin we were taken to watch Juventus, who shared a stadium with their city rivals. Juve were taking on Wolves in the UEFA Cup quarter-finals and it was the first time I'd seen an Italian team in the flesh as well the first time we had seen the stadium, a big bowl of a ground with a running track around the perimeter. Wolves held their hosts to a 1–1 draw, which in itself was a confidence boost for us, as we could see the Italians could be tamed.

It was a timely introduction to what we would be up against, not that we had been left in any doubt by the manager. When we ran out to play Torino we were as well drilled as I can ever remember being. We came away with a 1–1 draw, with Willie Johnston scoring the goal, and were confident that by making it home with the tie all square we had done the hardest part.

There was still the game at Ibrox to take care of and it was another tight affair. I can remember crossing for Alex MacDonald to score the only goal of the game and in that split second thinking we could go all the way. It was a huge breakthrough. The crowds had a huge part to play in that campaign. The European nights at Ibrox were magnificent, with the ground jam packed for every home tie.

When we got through to face Bayern there's no doubt it was a daunting prospect. Aside from two Polish players, they were not far off being the German national side in club form. The same German national side that went on to win the World Cup just two years later, which speaks volumes for the quality we had in our own side.

In the first leg in Germany we experienced a hammering of the type I've never suffered in my life. They came at us with wave after wave of attacks, relentless pressure. I was playing against

Paul Breitner, who was in at left-back, and vividly remember he played a one-two past me, flew up the park and scored from close range to put Bayern 1–0 up. I dived in like a wee boy, but I learned my lesson. For the remainder of the game we had to dig deep to keep them at bay and got our own reward when Willie Johnston's ball into the box was turned into the Munich net by Zobel. They had dominated in terms of possession but with the spirit and determination we showed we came away with a draw – and that all important away goal into the bargain. I would go as far as to say that result was one of the best ever achieved by a Scottish team in Europe.

Dave Smith was magnificent on a night on which the bulk of the game was played in our half. Cool heads were just as important as big hearts in that tie and the 1–1 result put us so near to the final – yet so far, given we had to face Bayern all over again. We hit a bit of form domestically going into the semi-final, but we were still huge underdogs. It was a case of the tables being turned for a group of players who spent most weekends playing as red-hot favourites.

What we were conscious of was the fact we carried a lot of expectation on our shoulders, regardless of who we were playing against. The supporters had been through the heartache of defeat in two European finals previously and we were desperate to ensure that didn't happen again. Aside from that, there was also the group of players – Sandy Jardine, Dave Smith, John Greig and Willie Johnston – who had been beaten by Bayern in the final of the competition in 1967 and they had more reason than most to make sure they didn't suffer that fate again. It had been close in '67 and was nip and tuck in '72. By the time Munich came to Glasgow for the second leg the stage was set. The costumes were taking shape too, with Adidas stepping in to kit us out for the semi-final. Looking back, I have to hope the club benefited from a sponsorship deal, but they certainly never let on at the time, perhaps concerned the players might look for a cut!

The problem was that none of us were too keen on wearing new boots. They are the tools of a player's trade and once you've worn a pair in you are loathe to change them, especially midway through a season like that. The solution was pretty simple: it was nothing a pot of paint and a brush couldn't sort. What we did was paint on the marks to make our existing boots look like Adidas versions with the three stripes. I wore Adidas in any case, but still didn't want to trade in my trusty old boots, and took my place in the queue to get the paint job done and make mine look like new. We were nothing if not inventive.

If you look back at photographs, particularly the team shot of us with the cup after we'd won the final, you'll notice we're all resplendent in our Adidas tracksuits and boots. It must have been the first sponsorship or kit deal that the club had ever had. Maybe Adidas realised they were on to a winner, because in the return match against Bayern we did ourselves and the supporters proud. The 2–0 win at Ibrox took us through to the final and sent the old ground into raptures. It was a phenomenal night and wonderful to be part of it.

Winning a place in the final, particularly when Bayern Munich stood in our way, gave us a real spring in our step. It would have been brilliant to have carried that momentum forward, but we actually hit a fairly substantial obstacle in the shape of the lay-off we had between our last league game on 1 May and the final on 24 May. Three weeks gave us a long period to try and keep ticking over and while the training was obviously upbeat, with a big Cup final around the corner, there's no substitute for match practice.

The games we played in the interim period were unusual, to say the least. There was one up at Inverness against a select side in a testimonial match and then a second against St Mirren in the

Paisley Charity Cup. It wasn't quite the same intensity we could expect out in Spain.

Between those two matches the whole squad were given a chance to play, with my turn coming up in the Highlands. I scored a couple of goals that day, one from the penalty spot, as we cantered to a 5–2 win in front of a very decent crowd at Grant Street Park. Alfie Conn and Andy Penman then came in for the second game, so from that point of view there was an opportunity for somebody to force their way ahead of me in the queue for a Cup final place. I'd staked my claim, all I could do was keep putting in the effort on the training field as the big game loomed.

The build-up was difficult in a sense – at home, wherever you went there were people wanting to talk about the final. In Barcelona that was even more intense, so we were isolated in the days leading up to the final to keep us away from the spotlight.

We had two training sessions while we were out in Spain, the rest of the time was spent back at the hotel. There were team meetings to attend, but the rest of the time was spent trying to kill time and prevent boredom setting in. There were meals and quizzes and the occasional walk, where we were greeted with supporters wishing us well and telling us, 'You have to win. You have to win.' The pressure was on!

In Barcelona there was an Under-21 game being played at the Nou Camp, so the traditional schedule of training in the ground on the eve of a tie went out the window. Instead we were at Espanyol's ground in what proved to be a horrendous session for Colin Jackson. When big Bomber was crocked during that final training stint it obviously threw the preparations into a bit of doubt. We were all gutted for Colin, who had been so important for us, and as far as the manager was concerned, it led to a rapid rethink.

That is when Derek Johnstone's versatility came into its own.

There were a few options available among the squad we had with us in Spain, but adding Derek to the starting eleven was the move I think we all expected. He had played in there before and had been very effective, and with plenty of experience throughout the team it didn't represent a big risk to take.

We had played 4-4-2 throughout that run, and Derek came in at the heart of the defence and was tasked with going to try and win every ball. In midfield, the big question mark surrounded Andy Penman and Alfie Conn. Both were vying for one jersey. With Derek taking the place of Colin, the rest of the team pretty much picked itself. I had been playing well and, although you never knew for sure, I was confident I'd be involved. From the Torino tie, the side had settled into a pattern and it was Waddell's old saying coming into play again: 'The more players, the more headaches.' He kept it simple, with very little chopping and changing.

We were desperate to do it for the supporters. It was a huge thing for them and they had turned out in their tens of thousands, spending a lot of money into the bargain, to back us. They deserved to go back to Glasgow as winners.

We knew very little about the Russians because of the obvious difficulties involved in getting reports on their matches, but Willie Waddell and Jock Wallace did their usual efficient job of preparing us as best they could. While we were idle, in competitive terms at least, Moscow Dynamo were in the middle of their season at that stage. The way the game at the Nou Camp panned out, it was easy to see how that changed the flow of the match – we got off to a flyer, but as time went on their extra match fitness began to tell and we faded. If it had gone to extra-time, we would have been in real trouble.

When you are three goals up and cruising, as we were, you feel in control. But as fatigue crept in we took a step back and brought problems upon ourselves, falling deeper and almost inviting them to attack us. We had shown against Bayern how resilient we could be and had to use those qualities against Dynamo that night. To go three ahead we had shown flair and passing ability. To keep it at 3–2 it was all about grit and sheer will to get over the finish line.

When the crowd came on to celebrate, it proved to be a false dawn. The terracing was just a step away from the pitch, so it wasn't surprising to see people spilling out onto the park. The final whistle brought them on again to celebrate. It was pure elation, but amid the mass of bodies it was a case of running hell for leather towards the tunnel. I can remember gasping for air – the humidity was incredible, a real hot and sticky evening in the Spanish summer – and with me hardly being a giant I was right in among it. Eventually I made it back to the dressing room, trying to take it all in – we'd done it.

There was obviously the carry on with the cup presentation in the aftermath, with John Greig getting spirited away to accept it in a back room, and we were all desperate to get back out on the pitch. But they simply wouldn't allow it. The Spanish police had over-reacted massively to the initial celebrations by the Rangers fans and the heavy-handed approach they took was the root of the problem, as far as I'm concerned. Had they been better prepared or had a little bit of foresight, it would all have passed off without a problem. Instead, decades later, we're still talking about the aftermath rather than the achievement itself.

Instead of parading around the Nou Camp, we did our celebrating deep within the stadium, getting the cup passed around and the champagne flowing. After the effort we put in and the amount we had sweated out over the course of the ninety minutes, the water and orange juice was being poured just as fast.

No matter what happened after the final whistle, they could

never take away what we had achieved in Barcelona, and very slowly it began to sink in that we had made a piece of Rangers history. It was pride, relief and joy all rolled into one. It was no fluke either. By beating the teams we had along the way to the final we had proved over and over again that we could live with the very best. At times we were criticised for a defensive approach, particularly by Rennes, but that told us we were doing our job. If the opposition were frustrated, it was always a good sign. The flip side was the praise we had from the likes of Rinus Michels along the way for the way we had gone about our business.

We had come quite a distance in a short space of time and for me personally it had been an incredibly quick year as I got to know a new set of players and their different characters. The special thing about the '72 team was the way those different characters came together as one. Bayern Munich arguably had better players individually, but as a unit we were superior. It was a privilege to be part of that group.

We had incredibly gifted players but we also had the natural Scottish tenacity and work ethic, something I think we all too often underestimate. Willie Waddell didn't want what I would call a 'one in four' type player – those who only play when the big games come around. He wanted people he could depend on week in and week out, rain or shine.

As a manager myself, I looked at the four As: ambition, ability, attitude and application. In terms of ambition, everyone wants to win. The big differential is how much they want it. With the other three, I would always put attitude and application ahead of ability, as without those qualities all the talent in the world is next to useless. I've always been willing to accept every player has a different level of ability, but you can't make any excuses if application is lacking.

What was unique about the Barcelona team was that we had

all four of those in abundance. We had the ability to score three very different goals and the ambition to do what no other Rangers team had managed to do, but without the application and right attitude we would not have seen it through to the final whistle that night.

I don't think the club has ever recognised the achievement properly. It has been left to the supporters, who have been fantastic, to do that. We defeated teams from France, Portugal, Italy, Germany and Russia, countries which don't tend to produce bad football teams. Can you imagine Scotland beating those nations to go on and win the European Championship? We would be shouting from the rooftops about that.

When we arrived back in Glasgow we were swamped by the fans – it meant so, so much to them. It wasn't the European Cup, but that didn't matter. Winning a European title was what was important and I'm proud to have played my part in that achievement. The memory of parading round Ibrox in the pouring rain with the European Cup Winners' Cup in our grasp will live with me forever. The hard work had been done in Barcelona and we arrived back with a sense of pure elation still sweeping through the squad. We had driven from Prestwick straight to the ground and ended up packing our bags in the dressing room, with everything bundled together when we left Barcelona in a bit of a spin. Then it was out on the back of the flatbed truck that features in so many of the photographs and out for the lap of honour. Everywhere we turned there were well-wishers ready to pat us on the back.

After the closed-door trophy presentation at the Nou Camp, back in Glasgow we were able to show off the cup and let the supporters join in the celebrations. For so many it was the first time they had caught a glimpse of the trophy and rain or no rain they were ready to raise the roof.

After the storm of the success and celebrations, the calm was not long in descending. I went home to Ashgill and there was one man waiting to greet me at the gate, a lad called Tom Ballentyne, who had been in my class at school. Other than that it was a quiet homecoming, quite surreal after everything that went before. You walk up the path just as you've done thousands of times before, bursting with pride but realising that life goes on win, lose or draw. It's a case of mixed emotions, really.

There was a reception dinner for us back in Glasgow before we all went our separate ways for the summer holidays, so it wasn't really until we got back for pre-season training that we caught up again and really had a chance to reflect on what had gone before. In truth the glory isn't long in passing as you're back into the familiar routine and starting all over again for the new season.

We had renewed confidence after the result against Dynamo but knew the hard work was just beginning. Beating the best in Europe was no guarantee of success domestically and there was certainly no complacency on our part. We were looking forward to rolling up our sleeves and preparing for another season, with Celtic in our sights. In practical terms, the win in Barcelona didn't alter anything for the players. Yes, we got a bonus for winning the cup but there were no bumper contracts on the back of it or anything like that. We were all on one-, two- or three-year contracts at the time and pretty much on a par as far as wages were concerned. We all had our basic pay topped up by appearance money and win bonuses, so to be earning decent wages you had to be in that team and doing well. It was the same at every club up and down the country – certainly no room for players to be sitting in the reserves making themselves millionaires. The only time I can remember that changing at all was after Sandy Jardine, Tam Forsyth and Derek Johnstone had been picked to go with Scotland to the World Cup in Argentina. They negotiated improved terms on the back of that and I was among the others to benefit from that with a similar deal.

It wasn't always as easy as that, mind you. On the back of the Treble in 1976 I remember going to Jock Wallace and telling him that if I wasn't getting an increase then I wanted away. Before long I was called up to Willie Waddell's office and before I could sit down was told, 'I hear you're looking for a move if you don't get more money? Put it this way: your transfer is granted.'

Needless to say, I never did push to get away and my wages didn't rise. In some ways I took a bit of comfort from that response because I knew that everyone else was getting the same treatment, there was no way those who shouted loudest would be getting preferential treatment when it came to the wage structure. It was there to be adhered to and helped underpin the all-for-one mentality.

There was a real sense of togetherness and it was a good environment to play in. Young players were given their chance, with Derek Johnstone and Alfie Conn given huge responsibility in Barcelona. Just as I was thrown in against Real Madrid by Kilmarnock as a teenager, there was a willingness to take a chance on youthful players. The bigger league helped that process domestically, with games in the eighteen-team set-up that allowed for a degree of experimentation. It also eliminated the monotony that smaller leagues breed and if we still had that it might have prevented the talent drain that we have seen in recent generations. You look at players of the quality of John Collins, who felt he had to get away from Scotland to alleviate the boredom of playing the same teams four, five or even six times every season depending on Cup draws. You can understand why players perhaps do not develop or stay stimulated when faced with that type of programme.

The two-points for a win also meant the gulf didn't open up so quickly if you were beaten, so that eased some of the pressure on both managers and players. All in all, it was a good environment for bringing younger players through. We'll obviously never go back to two-points and I wouldn't suggest we do, but I do think there are lessons we can take from the era in which a steady stream of world-class players were being produced in Scotland and England. We had Denis Law, Billy Bremner, Kenny Dalglish and many more in relatively quick succession and I don't see any reason we can't get back to that with the right approach.

Don't get me wrong, I'm not suggesting that we will see our club sides enjoying European success. We are so far behind that making up ground seems impossible, but what we should be able to do is unearth some individual gems who are capable of going out to the best leagues in the world and flying the flag for Scotland. It has been done in other countries of similar size and the young players are the lifeblood of our game. We can manipulate the leagues and try different formulas, but the key to improving the product is creating an environment where young players are given an opportunity to play with the freedom to express themselves. For that to happen there has to be a big change of mindset, although already we are seeing signs of some clubs taking the bull by the horns and making that change.

Money is important, in terms of infrastructure and facilities, but attitude is paramount to making progress. There has to be a serious commitment at all levels of the game to putting the development of players at the top of the agenda and a consistent approach from grassroots level right the way through to the very top. It might mean short-term pain for some clubs, but in the long-term everyone will reap the rewards.

8

WORDS OF WISDOM

It would be a Saturday night when the phone would ring. The gruff voice at the other end was a familiar one – Mr Waddell. Long after his involvement on the frontline of football had ended and my own managerial career had begun, my old boss would regularly get in touch to chew the fat. More often than not the late-night calls would come when my back was to the wall and my team was going through a rough patch. He was obviously watching from a distance and ready to swing into action when required.

Quite frequently those telephone conversations would develop into real ding-dong battles between the two of us – him cursing and snarling at me, and the pleasantries flowing in the opposite direction. It was the result of two strong-minded, some might say stubborn, characters getting together to discuss the finer points of management. They wouldn't be short calls either – when Beth picked up the phone at home and it was Mr Waddell on the other end, she knew not to expect me to be free for the rest of the evening. Without fail I'd put the phone down having gained something from the debate, something I could use to my advantage. Waddell was a man who knew his football.

Sometimes when you're going through a difficult spell the last thing you want to hear is the truth, but that was what he did best. I'd argue that I knew exactly what I needed to do to turn my team around, but bemoan the fact I had no money to do it. In response he'd trot out his favourite line: 'The more players you have, the more headaches they bring.'

I didn't like to admit it too often, but he was right. While I'd be pining for funds to bring in new faces, he'd be telling me quite simply: 'Stop complaining and do something about it. You have to work with what you've got, manipulate it from within.'

I did that time and time again, and he was right. Nine times out of ten, with a bit of imagination and hard work in equal measure, there were ways and means of getting more from a group of players than you ever thought possible. I didn't have the luxury of discarding players who perhaps weren't doing the job I wanted. I had to keep trying them in different positions until I found one that worked. From that point of view, Waddell was quite right, manipulating the squads I had at my disposal became the most important skill I ever employed in management.

The relationship I had with Waddell was a special one. He knew me inside out, knew my character. Because of that, when he thought I needed a pep talk he'd be straight on the phone telling me, 'I can imagine you sitting there with your wee face tripping you; it's time you came out fighting.'

The remarkable thing about it was that I'd only actually spent two years with Waddell as my manager, one at Kilmarnock and one at Rangers. No sooner had he signed me at Ibrox than he was planning his exit from the manager's office.

The dust had barely settled on our success in Barcelona in 1972 when The Deedle, as he was known, announced his decision to step down from the top job. As players, we had been given absolutely no indication that changes were afoot. Really I should have been the one to have seen the writing on the wall. After all, I'd seen it before at Kilmarnock when we won the league in what was to be Waddell's final game in charge. The difference at Killie was that the intention to resign had been made clear early in the season, whereas at Rangers it wasn't until after the win at the Nou Camp that the news was announced.

So there it was: two years under Mr Waddell's tutelage and I had a League Championship winner's medal and a matching one from the European Cup Winners' Cup. He seemed to have the Midas touch, everything clicked into place during those seasons. Whether he thought that was as good as it would get, I'm not sure. There's no doubt that the Barcelona team probably hit its peak during that run, with one or two in the latter stages of their career and others sold while their stock was high. That left the prospect of some rebuilding work in the years ahead for whoever was in charge. Maybe Waddell felt that was a job better suited to a younger man, as I certainly don't think there was any pressure on him to move aside. I suppose you sit and think 'that's me had my fill' – it was his third year at Rangers, he had the European trophy in the bag and must have been wondering if it could get any better.

If the decision by Waddell to let go of the reins was a surprise, the appointment of Jock Wallace as his successor was anything but. Even when he was second in command, it was Jock who had more involvement with the players on a day-to-day basis. From that point of view, nothing would change moving forward.

With Waddell moving on to a general manager's role, there was also still the suspicion that he would continue to pull the strings. He was still around the ground every day, although never in the dressing room. If there were any contract issues to be discussed, Waddell was the man. He was a tough negotiator too, so that side of the business was in very safe hands. Very quickly after Barcelona the team began to break up Willie; 'Bud' Johnston and Colin Stein were sold on. In Bud's case it was a chance to get himself out of the firing line after a few brushes with the SFA's disciplinary panel and with Colin the club decided to cash in its chips and take the profit when Coventry came calling with an open chequebook. Both came back in later years, so obviously still had a lot left in the tank. Those were sudden departures, but the fact both returned in later years shows it wasn't personal. It was simply a changing of the guard.

The club had lost the two men who had scored the goals in the Barcelona final and the real challenge was to make sure their absence didn't wash away all of the good work that had been done up to that point. Just as Bud and Colin Stein had moved on, Dave Smith and Willie Mathieson were also allowed to move on within a season or two and Wallace, alongside Waddell, had his work cut out to start filling those voids and looking to the future. Derek Johnstone was coming more and more to the fore, with his impressive versatility so crucial to us, and Quinton Young showed all the requirements of being a successful Rangers player after heading north as part of the deal which took Steiny to Coventry.

But Jock still had a team to build and what most people looking in from the outside would not be aware of is the fact he did it on a shoestring, relatively speaking. Quite rightly, the resources were being directed at the reconstruction of the stadium, which had become a quest for Waddell in the aftermath of the Ibrox disaster. It was still a huge influence on life at the club and always will be. Waddell felt a duty to the families of the sixty-six who lost their lives supporting the club and although I had joined the club afterwards, we all shared that feeling. The money for the stadium redevelopment was being pulled together behind the scenes and the work began to take shape. It made Ibrox a strange place to play at as the stands were taken down and the new ones appeared in their place – not least when the traditional Rangers end came down.

The challenge through that period of change was to find a way to compete with Celtic without being able to match them pound for pound. Whereas in the years leading up to Barcelona there had been substantial investment in the squad, including the £100,000 purchase of Colin Stein as well as the addition of the likes of Alex MacDonald and myself, the new focus ensured the policy had shifted. Younger players were being brought through the system and those who did come in from outside were the result of some serious wheeling and dealing rather than simply dipping into the bank account.

Jock had to be inventive and set about his work with typical passion. He was a good guy. He had his famous fitness regime but everyone from the outside looks upon Jock Wallace as some sort of brute – but there was a softer side to the man. Yes, he hammered us in pre-season and gave us some horrible sessions. But during the season itself we actually had a civilised existence, able to fall back on the great core fitness we had built through hard graft in the summer. Generally the routine would be a light session on a Monday to loosen the muscles, another light session on Tuesday and then often a game on the Wednesday. If that was the case, we'd be given a day off on a Sunday and then come back in for another light session. The lesson was that a good base of fitness stays with you. If you put yourself through the mill in those early stages then the rest falls into place. I can say with certainty that we were never found wanting in the latter stages of a game, able to dig deep and call upon the reserves that had been built up.

We called upon all of that inner steel in the 1974/75 season, the year in which we set out to stop Celtic making it ten-in-a-row. It was only a number, but it meant so much more to everyone connected to Rangers.

There was massive pressure on us to win the league, both from within the dressing room and from the supporters on the terraces. We thrived under that pressure and came through in style. There was no doubt we were closing the gap on Celtic, even with their conveyor belt of young talent. Kenny Dalglish was emerging as a major player for them and they still had quality right the way through the team with the likes of Danny McGrain and Lou Macari also emerging. We had quality too, but we also had the extra edge that year. Put simply, we wanted it more.

Of course, in the final shake-up it was Hibs, who were our closest challengers that year as Celtic had to be content with third spot. When Colin Stein scored to clinch the title when we drew 1–1 with Hibs at Easter Road, with four games to spare, it sparked the most incredible celebrations. The supporters partied in Edinburgh, partied on the road back home and kept that party going in Glasgow. The sense of relief, excitement and sheer jubilation was a joy to behold.

From a personal point of view, it had been one of the most satisfying seasons I had ever had. I played in all but one of the thirty-four First Division matches – missing a 3–2 win against Partick in only the second week of the campaign – and hit a rich vein of form in front of goal. In fact, I wasn't far off topping the scoring chart and finished just three goals behind Derek Parlane at the top of the leader board.

Derek chipped in with seventeen goals, so my own tally of fourteen was no mean feat for me coming from a deeper position. There were some memorable goals in among that batch, including the winner in a hard-fought 2–1 win up at Aberdeen and the same again when we beat Hearts 2–1 at Ibrox. I scored against Celtic at home too, the middle goal in a 3–0 victory, and bagged a hat-trick at Dumbarton the following week. That was something of a collector's item for me, and although goal scoring is part of any midfielder's make-up it certainly hadn't been a huge part of my game up to that season. Derek Johnstone matched my fourteen goals, so of the eighty-six goals we scored throughout that winning league season, more than half of them came from the two Dereks and me.

That was my fourth season as a Rangers player and represented my third trophy. After the European Cup Winners' Cup in 1972 came the Scottish Cup success the following year. It is difficult to put into words the thrill of playing in front of more than 120,000 supporters in an Old Firm Cup final, never mind what it feels like to win it. That was exactly what we did in the 1973 final, coming through with a 3–2 victory thanks to the efforts of Derek Parlane, Alfie Conn and big Tam Forsyth in front of goal. That was Tam's final, of course, and if anyone deserved that moment of glory it was him.

I did my bit to help us on the road to Hampden playing all six ties. Our fourth-round tie against Hibs had gone to a replay at Easter Road and I got both of the goals in our 2–1 in Edinburgh, one of them from the penalty spot. We had scraped past Dundee United in the previous round and went on to beat Airdrie 2–0 in the quarter-final and winning by the same margin against Ayr United in the semi-final. By the time we faced up to Celtic in the final we knew the destiny of the league trophy, and it was Parkhead rather than Ibrox. We had gone within a whisker of winning the title, ending up losing it by just a single point. We had lost just four games all season in the league, but still, it wasn't enough. That was painful, to say the least, so to win the cup was at least some consolation to us.

The near misses we had in the championship made finishing top of the pile in 1975 all the sweeter. The amount of physical and emotional effort we had invested in stopping ten-in-a-row could have had an impact and after the highs of that title win the danger was that we would fall flat the following year. But there was no chance Jock Wallace would let that happen. He was like a dog with a bone as he set about re-establishing Rangers as the dominant force.

The first of two Trebles we won under Jock, in 1975/76, sent out the message loud and clear that we were a club leading the pack. The fact it was the first year of the Premier Division made it even more special, it felt like being the first name on the trophy was symbolic of our intentions for the years ahead. The switch from an eighteen-team league to a division of ten had been a huge talking point before the changes were made. The intention was to provide more meaningful games, although it did lead to the repetition of playing each team four times a season rather than twice. You soon got used to that element, and in the main, the restructuring did revitalise the Scottish game.

St Johnstone hadn't read the script though, relegated after winning just three games all season in the new all-singing all-dancing Premier Division, but the five teams above them were separated by just three points so the idea of ensuring more competition had born fruit, with Dundee the other team dropping down after a real scrap among a clutch of teams to avoid that dreaded ninth spot. Our concern was at the other end of the table and with the advent of the new system and the prospect of four Old Firm games in the league, the matches against Celtic took on even greater significance.

The Premier Division opened with a derby – the wonders of the fixture computer! With all eyes on us, we won 2–1 to get the ball rolling. We went undefeated in the Old Firm matches that term, drawing 1–1 at Parkhead in the next encounter and then winning the second Ibrox fixture 1–0. By the time we went to their place in the penultimate match of the season we were already champions and came away with a 0–0 draw to ensure the gap wasn't closed. We ended up with a six-point cushion, exactly the number we'd won against Jock Stein's team from a possible eight. The last match in the Premier Division programme had us at home to Dundee United, a day later than the rest of the clubs had completed their fixtures. For the McLeans, it proved to be a day of celebration for very different reasons.

With the title already in the bag, we arrived at Ibrox for that match as Treble winners. The Scottish Cup final had been played three days earlier at Hampden and we had beaten Hearts 3–2 in a cracking match, with big DJ and Alex MacDonald scoring the goals. Doddie had scored the only goal of the game in the League Cup final against Celtic in October to get us off and running on the Treble trail, so there was a bit of symmetry about him rounding things off in the Scottish Cup. That was famously the game in which DJ had scored the opener before 3pm – with the referee starting a couple of minutes early and Derek scoring with a header from a chipped free kick I had played into the box in our first attack of the game.

After so many lean years, to have won back-to-back championships and the Treble into the bargain was like a dream come true for the players and the supporters alike. Running out at Ibrox for the last game of that season, we felt like kings. There were 50,000 there to welcome us and it was a real party atmosphere – but we had a job to do first. For my brother Jim and his Dundee United team it a was a huge occasion too. They went into the match in ninth place, staring relegation in the face. They were only a point off Dundee in eighth but the odds were stacked against them.

There was certainly no question of us taking our foot off the pedal. If we could have stretched our lead over Celtic in second place it would have been an even better season from our point of view. But Jim had his troops well drilled, we huffed and puffed but couldn't find a way past them. Our visitors had the best chance of the game when they were awarded a penalty kick, but Hamish McAlpine, their goal-scoring goalkeeper, missed from the spot and had to get himself back down the park sharply.

It finished 0–0 and, by virtue of a superior goal difference, that point was enough to take United out of the relegation zone and to safety. It was last gasp stuff, but I knew what it meant to our Jim – a massive weight lifted from his shoulders when that final whistle sounded. If they had been relegated at that point they would have had to sell some of the best young players to survive, so the likes of Paul Sturrock, David Narey, Ralph Milne and John Holt would have been moved on. It proved to be a turning point for them, with United pushing back up the table in the years ahead and proving a force in the top half as they built towards the championship win in 1983. It just goes to show how fine the margins are, how important every single point can be.

Jim and I seemed destined to share the major moments that season, with our own championship win coming up at Tannadice less than a fortnight before the return fixture at Ibrox. It was another close affair, with Derek Johnstone's goal the only thing separating us. DJ was a big Dundee United supporter as a boy and all his family followed the club, so those games were always special for him. It would have hurt him to see them go down, but he was a Rangers man and winning was all that mattered when he had a blue shirt on his back. We had a huge travelling support up with us in Tayside that day and they went back down the road a happy bunch.

The Treble was the ultimate reward for years of loyal support. Rangers will always be judged on how they perform against Celtic domestically and that season it was 3–0 when it came to the trophy count. It was perfect.

As much as anything, getting over the finish line that season was a relief to the players. We had worked so hard week in and week out and were desperate to prove we were the dominant force. There may have been better individual players around in the Scottish game during that period and Jock Wallace did not have the luxury of being able to go out and buy them, but as a unit we were formidable. One for all and all for one – that was the key to success.

9

LOOKING TO THE FUTURE

To win a Treble as a player is an incredible experience. To win two is something dreams are made of. The 1977/78 season was when that became a reality, on the back of our clean sweep just two years earlier. Comparing the Treble-winning seasons is difficult, but the one in '78 was perhaps the most significant because it represented the pinnacle for a group of players who largely had been together through thick and thin for the best part of a decade. It was the last season before that team began to break up, so it was all the more special to have swept the boards. It was, of course, also notable because it was Jock Wallace's swansong, even if we didn't know that at the time. By the time the next season kicked off, it was the blue of Leicester City, not Rangers, that his players were wearing.

We never heard a whisper about the prospect of Jock moving on until the announcement was made in the summer of 1978. To say we were in shock would be an understatement, especially after the season we had just had. You don't tend to lose your manager on the back of a Treble, but that's the position we found ourselves in.

Rewinding back twelve months, all of the signs were that long-term plans were being put in place. Lowering the average age of the team appeared to be at the top of the agenda, with

Bobby Russell emerging as a key man and the £100,000 investment in Davie Cooper from Clydebank demonstrating the willingness at board level to spend big to attract the best young talent. Davie was twenty but was an old head on young shoulders, such a clever football player. Gordon Smith, who was just twenty-two at the time, had also been brought in at the start of the 1977/78 season and Jock's message was clear: The old guard couldn't afford to be complacent. He wanted competition for places right the way through the team and the combination of new signings and players being pushed through from the reserves certainly gave an extra edge going into that season.

The energy the young recruits gave us added a spark, but the experience right through the core of the team was a major part in what we did. The likes of Peter McCloy, Sandy Jardine, Tom Forsyth, Colin Jackson, John Greig, Alex MacDonald, Derek Johnstone and myself had all been over the course before and knew what it took to go the distance. Winning the Treble takes a lot of different qualities – resilience, stamina and concentration among them. One lapse, one slip and the dream can be killed stone dead. If you don't have the balance of youth and experience the chances are substantially reduced.

The league was always the priority, and we didn't get off to the best start. We went up to Aberdeen on the opening day of the season and lost 3–1 then were beaten 2–0 by Hibs at Ibrox the following week. Far from setting the pace, we were rock bottom of the Premier Division and playing catch-up on Aberdeen as they stole a march. Billy McNeill was in charge at Pittodrie and putting together a talented and hungry young team, bringing in the likes of Gordon Strachan and Steve Archibald along the way. They made a wonderful start and for the first couple of months looked like the team to beat, an early sign of what was to come in the years ahead.

Our first win of the season actually came in the League Cup, when St Johnstone came to Ibrox in the second round. We won 3–1 but it was a comfortable night's work and a good boost to the confidence. We took that into the league with us and went on a fifteen-game unbeaten run. Aberdeen came to Glasgow during that spell and we were worthy 3–1 winners, overtaking them to go top on the back of that result.

With Celtic toiling, it turned out to be a straight fight between ourselves and the Dons for the title and it was nip and tuck right the way to the finish line. We led for large swathes of the campaign but a blip in the last quarter, when we lost to Celtic and dropped points against Hibs, St Mirren and Ayr United, let Aberdeen sneak back in front.

With three games to play we were tucked in behind and faced a difficult run-in, with a double-header against Dundee United home and away then Motherwell at Ibrox on the final day of the season. Jim's team were pushing for third place, which would have been the highest they had ever finished, so there was everything to play for. It turned out to be a happy ending for both McLeans – we beat them at Tannadice in midweek, with a goal from Derek Johnstone the only thing separating the teams, and then won 3–0 at home three days later. The plus point was United went on to take third spot in any case.

By the time we went into the Motherwell game we were top of the table and knew a victory was enough to wrap up the title – and we finished the job, running out 2–0 winners. With Aberdeen only drawing at Hibs, we ended with a two-point margin after what had been a long, hard and incredibly competitive championship race.

Derek Johnstone was on tremendous form, scoring twenty-five goals in the league alone, and was quite rightly named Player of the Year by the Scottish Football Writers' Association and the Scottish Professional Footballers Association. It was fitting that Derek scored the winner in the Scottish Cup final the week after the league had been won, with Aberdeen the opponents at Hampden. The League Cup was already back in the trophy cabinet, having beaten Celtic 2–1 in the final, and we beat the Dons by the same score line in the Scottish Cup to clinch the Treble. Including four ties in the European Cup Winners' Cup that season, we played fifty-three matches. I played in all but nine of those but can honestly say that fatigue was never a factor for anyone in that dressing room. When you are successful and there are trophies to be won, the energy reserves run that little bit deeper.

When the celebrations subsided after the Cup win, rounding off the Treble, we left for the summer break in great spirits. We had a European Cup campaign to look forward to and everything was rosy in the garden. Then, just over a fortnight after the big day out at Hampden, the news broke that Jock had resigned. He was forty-two, still a young man, but already had two Trebles under his belt, something no other Rangers manager had ever achieved. It marked him out as one of the most successful coaches in the British game, with his role in the European success in 1972 giving him another impressive addition to his CV. It is easy to see why he was a man in demand, although at the time I don't think anyone – including the Rangers board – really thought he would consider moving on. But he did, and it caught everyone on the hop.

The manager's departure marked a turning point for Rangers and Scottish football in a sense. It was an indication that finance was starting to take over, with Jock getting his offer from Leicester and Rangers couldn't, or wouldn't, match it. That would have hurt him because he loved the club, but sometimes you have to put yourself first in the most precarious of occupations.

Just as managers were having their heads turned, players too were starting to attract interest from the first of the football agents. I always handled my own affairs as a player. My only contact with an agent was when Bill McMurdo tried to get me to move to Hibs. I didn't take that any further, but there was no doubt that the face of football was changing. The advent of the agents was the first sign of business taking priority, whereas before the game had always come first.

Leicester, a Second Division club, demonstrated with what was a bold move that no manager or player was off limits for English clubs with resources at their disposal. I don't for a second think that money was the only motivation. From a football perspective, Leicester represented a massive challenge. They had just been relegated but had huge potential and clearly the opportunity to take on that project was one that the manager was ready to embrace.

When it happened we were away from the club during the close-season break, so it was even more surreal. It was front-page news and it felt almost as though we were looking in from the outside as it all unfolded. As soon as it became clear Jock was leaving, the newspapers began to speculate about who would succeed him. John Greig was at the top of most of the lists but Alex Ferguson, who had done a good job with St Mirren, and Ally Macleod, busy preparing for the World Cup in Argentina, were also mentioned. Those names may have helped make a few headlines but in actual fact I don't think there was ever any doubt about the man who would take charge. John Greig had served his apprenticeship as a player and captain, through good times and bad, and it was his time. It always felt a case of when, rather than if, he would take on the top job – it wasn't a surprise to anyone in the dressing room.

The appointment was swift and decisive, which, from a

player's point of view, was encouraging. Had there been a period of uncertainty in between then it may have been more unsettling, but the fact is that we knew very quickly how things were going to pan out.

Given the success we had just enjoyed, with the Treble in the bag, it would have been an impossible task for somebody to come in from the outside and be seen as anything other than second best. Back-to-back Trebles was always a long shot. The benefit John had was his track record as a player and the support of the fans, meaning there would be a bit of breathing space. Celtic had a new manager too, in the shape of Billy McNeill, so the face of the Old Firm was changing. They had been opponents so often on the park and now they were in opposite dugouts.

When we went back to training in July 1978 it was different for the players and different for John, there's no doubt about that. It was still a pre-season that we recognised, but Greigy was putting his own stamp on things from early on. On that first day back he gathered us together after the morning's training and spoke from the heart about his aims for the season ahead. We were on a high after the Treble and it was a rallying call as much as anything – more of the same was what was required.

There hadn't been a huge amount of time for him to plan or find his feet, but he had the benefit of knowing us all inside out and being able to lean upon the work Jock had done in the previous years. We were a well-drilled squad, so in that respect it made the job easier in those early weeks and months.

Unfortunately for John, we were also an ageing squad. From the moment he accepted the manager's job he quite rightly bowed out of playing, so that was the first casualty in squad terms. There were quite a few others at that time, myself included, who had been at the club for many years and clearly couldn't go on forever. Peter McCloy, Sandy Jardine, Alex

MacDonald ... the list goes on. Jock had undoubtedly had the best years out of us and had reaped the rewards with the trophies we had won, including the two Trebles. Don't get me wrong, he had to wheel and deal on a relatively limited budget to maintain the squad, but what Greigy faced was a rebuilding job.

The record books show that there were mixed results, with success and some frustration. With hindsight he would probably say himself that he moved Alex MacDonald on too quickly. Sandy Jardine was a slightly different case, as he moved to join Alex at Tynecastle, but when you look at what he did in a maroon shirt in the years that followed it was clear he still had a lot to offer.

What we also had to contend with that we hadn't up to that point was a threat from a new direction in the shape of Aberdeen and Dundee United. Up to that point it had been very much a two-horse race for the title in my time at the club, but the emergence of the Dons under Alex Ferguson and United under our Jim had thrown things wide open. All of sudden we found ourselves going toe to toe with teams that were young, energetic and being driven forward by two incredibly ambitious and intelligent managers. The talent in the Aberdeen and Dundee United squads at that time was impressive and the majority of those players were home-grown, products of impressive youth systems. To be fair to John, he recognised the importance of getting the youth structure right and devoted time and energy to that, but as an Old Firm manager time is never a luxury you are afforded. He needed a quicker fix than that and set about shuffling his pack.

One of his first tasks after taking over was to persuade Derek Johnstone to stay with the club. Derek had requested a transfer whilst Jock Wallace was still in charge but had a change of heart after talking things through with John and was appointed captain for the start of the new season. Alex Forsyth was taken in on loan from Manchester United, and before that, Billy Urquhart was bought from Inverness Caledonian. Forsyth was viewed as the first-choice left-back but ended up being replaced by young Ally Dawson midway through the season, the start of Ally's rise to prominence and another sign of John's willingness to give promising boys their chance in the first team.

Although the changes early on were minimal, unfortunately the results did not match the form we had shown the previous year. We went half a dozen games in the Premier Division without winning a match from the start of the season, languishing in the bottom half of the table. After the highs of the Treble, it was a real test of character for John and the squad. I didn't doubt we would turn the corner and it took a big occasion to kick things into gear. We had been drawn against Juventus in the European Cup first round and lost 1–0 in Italy in the first leg, a game I sat out as Alec Miller came in to play a more defensive role against Antonio Cabrini. Not too many people gave us a chance after that result in Turin but we turned the tables on them in Glasgow.

It was another incredible European night at Ibrox against a Juve team with nine Italian internationals in the starting eleven. John brought me back in for that game and I had plenty of joy down the right side that night and it was a game, one I really savoured. We scored either side of half-time through Alex MacDonald and Gordon Smith and that 2–0 win must rate as another one of the great Rangers results.

We hoped that performance would reflect in the league results but in truth we never really hit top gear. The disappointing thing is that even without putting together a consistent run of wins in the Premier Division, we still managed to claw our way to the top of the league at one stage. We drew nine of our thirty-six fixtures and if we had managed to edge just one or two of those games we would have gone on to win the league. In the end we finished runners-up to Celtic, three points adrift.

The title had come down to an Old Firm match at Parkhead in the third-last game of the season. Celtic had endured a miserable start to the season but came good in the final furlong. We needed at least a draw at their place to stay on course for the title and we looked to be in the box seat when Alex MacDonald put us ahead. Celtic had John Doyle sent off in the second half and at that stage the title looked to be heading back to Ibrox. Then it started to slide. They went 2–1 ahead through Roy Aitken and George McCluskey. Bobby Russell levelled things back at 2–2 but a Colin Jackson own goal and Murdo McLeod's late goal gave Celtic the two points and put paid to our own hopes. It was a horrible, horrible way to see the championship slip away.

The 1978/79 season held painful memories for me in more ways than one. The problems had started for me right at the start of our Scottish Cup run, when I'd first started to struggle with a niggling ankle injury. I was getting a few injuries at that time, but it was obvious this was more than just a passing problem. It turned out to be calcification of the bone and I was given quite a few cortisone injections to get me through games. I can remember being laid out in the showers getting a jab and it certainly worked to numb the pain. Effectively what was happening was the bone from my heel was pushing into my Achilles tendon when I pushed down on it, giving me a real jolt with pain when I took a step. Cortisone was the main treatment being used for a whole raft of injuries at that time. We know now the impact too much cortisone can have and the difficulties some people have had in later life, but I'm one of the fortunate ones and, touch wood, have stayed fit.

We weren't aware of the potential for problems, but even if we had been I'm not convinced it would have changed attitudes.

When you're getting injections to kill the pain before you've even started a game, you know deep down it isn't the best course of action, but playing was our livelihood. No game meant no appearance money and no bonus. To be paid well you had to be out on the park and doing well.

By the time we played the Scottish Cup final, I was toiling. The doctors had decided I needed surgery and had booked me in for an operation at the Victoria Hospital when the season ended – unfortunately it was the season that didn't want to end. We played Hibs in the final and drew 0–0, so went to a replay four days later. Again, we couldn't produce a goal between us and it went to a second replay another twelve days later. By the time we won that last game 3–2 I would have been glad to have walked to the hospital myself.

The best thing about it all was that they got it all over and done with in time for me to watch Nottingham Forest beat Malmo in the European Cup final on the TV – that was my one instruction to the medics: I wanted to be out of theatre and comfortable for the match. There was a nagging feeling that we should have been playing in that match rather than watching it. After beating Juventus in the first round we didn't fear anyone left in the draw. PSV Eindhoven were the team we were paired with next and we pulled another great performance out of the bag over in Holland, winning 3–2 after drawing 0–0 at Ibrox in the first leg.

We tackled Cologne in the quarter-finals and despite losing 1–0 in Germany, we still fancied our chances of progressing when we faced them in the return on home soil. Unfortunately the opposition hadn't read the script and when they scored an away goal and went 2–0 ahead on aggregate we were left facing an uphill task. I chipped in with a goal to level it at 1–1 on the night late in the game, a cheeky free kick when their goalkeeper was still lining up the wall. It gave us a glimmer of hope, but was too late unfortunately.

There were fellow survivors from the '72 run involved in that game – Peter McCloy, Sandy Jardine, Colin Jackson, Alex MacDonald, Derek Johnstone and Derek Parlane – so we had the experience to fall back on. We genuinely thought we were good enough to go all the way to another final, but just fell short.

Our Cup form, not just in Europe, had been good. As well as beating Hibs, eventually, in the Scottish Cup final we lifted the League Cup too. We beat Celtic in the semi-final and then Aberdeen in the final, so it was far from an easy passage. At any normal club, a Cup double and reaching the quarter-finals of the European Cup wouldn't be a bad outcome. But Rangers is no normal club – the expectations are huge. The league is the benchmark and the comparison to Celtic is the key. No prizes for second place and the fact they were the one team above us made it all the more disappointing.

John went back to the drawing board and was backed by the directors with some money to spend, although far from a king's ransom. Gregor Stevens came in for a six-figure fee and John McDonald was pushed into the first team. The rebuilding continued and the rest is history that doesn't make for happy reading. Results, in the main, were hugely disappointing. We finished the 1979/80 season empty-handed, and although there were wins in the Scottish Cup and League Cup in the next couple of years, I was starting to take a back seat and missed those two finals. The Treble of '78 proved to be among my final winner's medals as a player, not what I had envisaged when we were celebrating that achievement. I went on to pick up another in the 1981 Scottish Cup, when Dundee United took us to a replay. I played in that first match and was on the bench as we ran out 4–1 winners at Hampden.

You don't ever want that success to end and deep down you also don't want to contemplate the fact you can't go on playing at the top level forever. The truth of the matter is nothing stands still in football – that can be the pitfall but it is also the beauty of the game. There's always another adventure around the corner.

10

A RELUCTANT COACH

Having already said I think it is true to say football is in my blood, maybe it would be safe to assume that football management is too. In actual fact, it wasn't my career of choice. I loved playing the game, revelled in every match I took part in. But having seen the stresses and strains Willie and Jim had endured as managers in their own right, I was far from convinced it was a route I wanted to go down.

It began to become a serious consideration during the 1981/82 season when I played no more than a dozen games in the first team at Ibrox. I knew my time in the Rangers side was drawing to a close and had to start looking to the future. For someone who had known nothing but professional football man and boy, it was a major crossroads for me. I'd been building towards my retirement for a couple of years, going down to the SFA coaching courses at Largs with Alex Miller to work towards our badges.

As a rule, Rangers and Celtic players didn't play a big part in those sessions, but Alex and I had made the decision to put ourselves through the qualifications and it proved to be a wise move. Andy Roxburgh was in charge of coach education for the SFA at that point and they would bring in YTS players for us to work with. The late John Hagart, who had been in charge at Hearts and was manager at Falkirk as well as assistant to Ally

MacLeod with Scotland at the '78 World Cup, was the man who put me through my paces and rubber stamped my certificates. You couldn't help but learn from experienced men like John, but you had to put the Largs courses in your own context. Like a driving test, once you have your licence it is up to you how much of what you have been taught you carry with you day to day. Different people would take different elements from those courses and put them into use in a way they saw fit. I know I found myself thinking that there were certain sections of the course that I would definitely replicate, but there were others that I knew instantly that I wouldn't.

What nobody did was follow everything the SFA decreed to the letter – that is a myth surrounding Largs that built up over a number of years, that it was producing coaches and managers to some sort of identikit. For someone like myself, having spent my entire playing career at just two clubs, it was an opportunity to see how different people did things and to share ideas. What I was well aware of was the fact that we were all under the microscope, and it wasn't a walk in the park by any means. When you're in among strangers you have to have the confidence to stand up and deliver training sessions confidently and efficiently, all the time trying to put your own stamp on things whilst using the framework you have been taught. Some thrive on being in the centre of things, others find it a bit more daunting. In those early days I was somewhere in between and realised that gaining my badges was crucial for my future.

Although I wasn't dead set on management, I had already started to get involved in coaching at Ibrox while I was playing. I'd take the youth teams for training during John Greig's tenure as manager and I enjoyed that involvement. What I hadn't expected was the invitation I got in the summer of 1982 to step up and become assistant manager to John, part of a reshuffle of the coaching staff that saw Joe Mason and Stan Anderson take the reserve side and Davie Provan concentrating on his role as chief scout. Even with my previous misgivings about management, I didn't hesitate in accepting. It's amazing how an offer like that can make your mind up.

It turned out to be not the only opportunity that would come my way that summer. Before the news of my appointment at Ibrox had been made public, Alex MacDonald sounded me out about the possibility of becoming his assistant at Hearts. I always got on well with Doddie and in any other circumstances would have been delighted to accept, but I'd already promised John I would take the job at Rangers. There were difficult times ahead for us at Ibrox, but I have never regretted for a second that decision. It was a great experience to work alongside him and so often in adversity you learn more than you ever can when everything is perfect.

My job was very much on the training field, but John was a hands-on manager. I was there to support him, but he was the main man. What it did offer me was a steep learning curve, both from watching what Greigy went through and in my own experiences in dealing with players. I'd gone from playing alongside the bulk of the squad to being on the other side of the fence as a coach, which took a bit of getting used to.

John had gone through the same process and, looking back, it was always going to be difficult for him in those circumstances at a club the size of Rangers. People look back on his time in charge as a failure in the grand scheme of things but it cannot be overlooked that he won trophies during a transitional period for the club.

Above all else, I would look back on his time in charge as being an unlucky one – both for him and for the club. It was unfortunate the way in which it all happened so quickly, with

John having to go into his first season with little time to prepare or take a step back and look to the future, and it was unfortunate in the way that so many good and experienced players were coming to the end of their playing days. There were such big voids to fill, with so little money to do it.

But do I think Greigy was wrong to take the job? Not for a moment. These are, usually, once in a lifetime opportunities – if he turned it down, there's a good chance it would never have been there for him again. So he had to give it a go.

There are many parallels between John's time in charge and Ally McCoist in more recent times. Ally knew, to an extent at least, that he was not taking the manager's job in the best circumstances but would never have forgiven himself if he had turned his back on the opportunity.

Of course, Ally couldn't have foreseen exactly how difficult it would become and the turmoil there would be behind the scenes. You need unity behind the scenes to have any chance of creating a team that is united on the park, something that has been sadly lacking in recent years. Similarly, John had to put up with a lot of in-fighting that made his job more difficult than it needed to be – with director Jack Gillespie making no secret of the fact he wanted someone else in the manager's chair and using his place on board to cause ructions. To me it appeared to be more about power than it was about moving the club or the team forward.

In the face of that, I think it would be wrong to level criticism at John. The only area where I do feel that he got it wrong was in not giving management another shot at a different club. He had such great knowledge of the game and experience, so it was a travesty that he was lost to the game when still a young man. I'm convinced he would have made an impact in management in the longer term if he had gone on, but he was Mr Rangers and clearly didn't feel comfortable going to work at another club. I respect that.

There were other positives to take from it, though. He left some very talented players behind – including Jim Bett, a wonderful playmaker, and a young Ally McCoist – and had also played his part in rearing some prospects for the future in the likes of Derek Ferguson. That work paid dividends further down the line and is all too easy to forget.

But John found himself caught in the middle of a power struggle behind the scenes. In the boardroom, Jack Gillespie was looking for change, whilst others on the board wanted to give the manager more time to try and turn things around. We knew what was going on and it felt like the clock was ticking, so when John eventually decided to walk away it wasn't a great surprise. He is the first to admit the pressure was taking its toll and when there's a split within any club it is an impossible situation. A clean break is the only way forward, a position I found myself in later in my own managerial career.

When the change was made, it threw my own position into a spin. It followed that a new broom would sweep clean, so I was staring at the prospect of unemployment for the first time in my life. It was obviously a worrying time, but the directors had asked me to stay in place and take charge of the team while they plotted the way ahead. What lay ahead was the small matter of a European Cup Winners' Cup tie against Porto on their turf.

We'd lost the first leg 2–1 at Ibrox while John was at the helm and recovering from that was always going to be difficult. I was new to management, if not coaching, and going in against one of the continent's big names in front of more than 60,000 passionate Portuguese supporters was not a bad test, to say the least. We lost that match 1–0 but I was quietly satisfied with the performance and the way we contained a very potent Porto side. We had chances to pull ourselves back into the tie, but didn't get the breaks. What it did do was whet my appetite for management. I'd had a taste and enjoyed it. Of course, I knew I wouldn't get the job on a permanent basis, no matter what had happened in that game or those against Celtic and St Mirren that I also took charge for. The wheels were already in motion to find an experienced pair of hands to take the tiller and I knew that at first hand.

Willie Thornton was very much Willie Waddell's right-hand man at Ibrox and it was Thornton who came to me and asked if I thought my brother Jim would be interested in the Rangers job. Without speaking to Jim, I said he would be. It began to gather pace after that and Jim certainly gave it careful consideration. It was a hard, hard decision for him to make. He had won the league with Dundee United the previous year and had built something special. Could he turn his back on that? He knew that if he turned down Rangers and they went in a different direction that my own position on the staff would be in jeopardy. Whoever came in would want his own assistant; there was no doubt about that. So from that point of view, Jim wasn't just making a decision about his own future but in effect had my destiny in his hands too. I was young and confident I could stand on my own two feet, so there was no pressure from me, but I know Jim felt a weight on his shoulders as he considered the implications.

Johnston Grant, the chairman at Dundee United at that time, had been like a father to Jim and had stood by him in the early part of his time as manager at Tannadice. He begged him to stay rather than go to Ibrox, and Jim certainly felt he owed him his loyalty. The decision was made, it was 'no' to Rangers and it was a P45 for me when Jock Wallace came in to take charge instead. Not for one moment did I hold that against Jim. He had to make the decision for himself and his family. In actual fact, even if Jim had accepted the job I would have taken a step back. He had spoken about taking Walter Smith with him from United and the likelihood is I would have been the reserve coach, which wouldn't have fazed me as I was just starting out.

There was certainly no regard for old times when Jock Wallace came in. I'd always got on well with him as a player, but he made it clear from day one that I didn't figure in his plans when it came to coaching.

The root of the problem appeared to be an interview I'd done with Alan Herron of the *Sunday Mail* while I was in interim charge at Rangers. I'd been quoted saying that I would like to be my own man, and Jock took umbrage with that, saying it would be difficult for him to keep me on when he knew that it could be a week, a month or a year until I moved on to take a job as a manager. I thought it was strange that he chose to bring up that newspaper article to justify the fact I was out on my ear, but I didn't find the decision itself surprising.

Fortunately in our profession you usually find that as one door closes, another opens. It wasn't long before I found myself back in work and on a winding path that brought me some wonderful experiences.

11

CAPPIELOW CALLING

When I walked out of Ibrox in 1983 I was stepping out into the big bad world. In football terms, I was an old hand – in the real world I was a young man with responsibilities but without a job. While I was hopeful something would quickly crop up, there was still a real fear factor. It was a new scenario for me and I did what I could to keep myself occupied, taking in as many games as I could.

It was that process that actually brought me my first break in management, with a visit to watch Dundee United play St Mirren bringing the type of twist of fortune that you need along the way. I bumped into the late Hal Stewart, who had managed Morton in the 1970s but by then was managing director of the club. It was around the time they were about to lose my old friend Alex Miller to St Mirren and there a vacancy opening up at Cappielow. It was very much a case of being in the right place at the right time as I must have been fresh in Hal's mind when he came to deciding on a successor to Alex and he invited me in for a meeting.

I drove down to the ground and within minutes I'd been offered and accepted the manager's job. It was November 1983 and it proved to be the beginning of the rest of my life, opening up a door into management when I had been worrying that I might be knocking for a long time before I got that chance. I saw it as a fantastic club to serve my apprenticeship with. Hugh Currie, with his commercial background in the shipbuilding industry, was the chairman but Hal was involved in the day-to-day running of the club. At that stage Hal claimed to be winding down and taking a backseat, but that was like our Jim saying he was taking a backseat. Hal was Mr Morton.

What I inherited from Alex Miller was a squad gunning for promotion from the First Division. Partick Thistle were leading the way, but Morton were on their coat tails and had a squad I was sure was equipped well for the chase. There wasn't money swilling around. In fact, the club was working with a fairly substantial overdraft, but the nucleus of a decent squad had already been assembled. My job was to pick up where Alex had left off and finish the job he had started.

On the day I agreed to take the job, the first team was scheduled to play Dumbarton away from home. I went along to the match, one we drew 1–1, but didn't go in before the game. Team affairs were left to Eddie Morrison, who had been coaching with Alex, but I did meet with the squad at full-time to introduce myself and get started with the task in hand.

Although I brought Tam Forsyth to Cappielow as my assistant, Eddie, who sadly died recently, was also part of the coaching team. I liked the continuity that brought and it was something I tried to do at every club I managed from then on in, retaining some of the experience and knowledge that existed within the ranks. It helped that I already knew Eddie, who had been a player at Kilmarnock as well as managing at Rugby Park. With Tam, he was a good friend during our time together at Rangers and was someone I trusted implicitly. He had gone back to his trade as a joiner after calling time on his playing days, so was available to come in and help out on a part-time basis.

The first few training sessions were a culture shock. For a large chunk of my career I'd been accustomed to the luxury of life at Ibrox, with our own training ground at the Albion to work from. Now I found myself having to scurry around looking for a patch of grass to train on at Gibbs Hill in Greenock or running sessions on a muddy corner of the turf at Cappielow, all the time trying not to cut up the pitch before we had to host a fixture on it. I also had to adapt to the peculiarities of part-time football. No sooner was I in the door than the phone calls started – the excuses for not being able to make the Tuesday or Thursday night training, with everything from work commitments to babysitting arrangements throwing my plans up in the air. I have to admit there were some I believed and others I was more sceptical about, but you've got little choice but to make the best of it and go with the flow.

Pretty soon I was developing my own style of management, although I have to admit there were some familiar McLean traits shining through. Both Willie and Jim, with their respective clubs, had made a point of directing any praise, criticism or observations directly at individuals rather than to a collective group – be it the defence, midfield or attack.

That was an approach I adopted myself, making sure there was never any ambiguity as to who I was addressing. I realised early on that communication was the most important tool in any manager's locker. Whether working with kids or senior professionals, if you can't get your message across then you're beaten before you start. Football is a simple game. I've always felt a manager's job is to simplify it even further, rather than complicate things. I've seen people tie themselves in knots by trying to impose systems or formations on players that simply aren't able to fit them. The players come first, the rest follows from the attributes they possess.

At Morton I took charge of a squad with a mixed bag of talents and varying levels of experience, but I have to admit I was pleased with what I found. Jim Duffy was there while Dom Sullivan was another with an excellent pedigree. There were the likes of Jim Holmes as well as the goalkeeper Murray McDermott. All at different stages in their career and from different backgrounds, but together an excellent unit. Most importantly, they were good professionals. As a young manager, that made my job a whole lot easier. I trusted them and in return they gave me the respect I needed to make my impression on the team.

I always recognised that boots and balls were the tools of the trade so I tried to ensure we did as much ball work as possible. Doing ten repetitions of a twenty-yard dribbling drill is the same as covering a 200-yard run, but ask any player what they'd rather do and they would tell you they'd go with the first option every time. I preferred to focus on short, sharp exercises when it came to fitness. We weren't trying to train marathon runners, so although stamina was obviously a factor, it was the explosive pace that could hurt the opposition that we really needed to hone.

We split the two evening training sessions into fitness-orientated work on a Tuesday and the tactical side on a Thursday. Nine times out of ten there would be call-offs to contend with, making it difficult to do the work on shape that I would have liked, but we grew accustomed to that particular challenge. It was all part of the role with a part-time club.

If I could have hand-picked a job, Morton would have been near enough perfect. As assistant manager at Rangers I had taken training, but I hadn't had the responsibility of picking the team or shaping the tactics. At Cappielow I was in a position where I could make the mistakes that anyone new to a job is likely to make but do it in an environment where I had room to grow and learn as I went along. It was good from the point of view that I could do that without losing faith or confidence in my own ability to deliver the goods, and I'd advise any young manager to follow a similar path. When you look at the experiences of John Greig at Rangers and Willie Miller at Aberdeen, two legends as players, you realise that going straight in at the top and under an intense spotlight is far from ideal.

Although it was a part-time job I had taken on, I appreciated that what I got out of the opportunity would depend on what I was willing to put in. I'd be down at the ground every day, dealing with everything from the mail to organising the scouting network and taking the YTS kids who played in the reserve league for us. The Youth Training Scheme, to give its proper title, wasn't introduced with football in mind – it was a means to get youngsters into work and save employers money on wages – but it was used by clubs up and down the land as a mechanism for employing teenagers and bringing them through. It was a case of treating football like any other 'trade'.

As the season took shape we were quietly but confidently building momentum. My first game in charge was at home to Airdrie and the players responded well, winning 3–2 to keep us in touch with Partick at the top. That result was a huge relief because the first impression is always the lasting impression and to get off and running with two points went a long way to easing me in to the manager's office. We kept plugging away through the winter and by the time Thistle came to Cappielow in February 1984 we were in touching distance of them. It was a rip-roaring game and we came away with a 4–2 win to hit first place for the first time since the opening day of the season. At that point the championship became a far more realistic target for everyone at the club.

It wasn't a straight gallop to the finish line, we dotted between first, second and third place over the months ahead, but we closed out the season with a nine-game unbeaten run and took the title. Dumbarton had come through to overtake Partick and took the second promotion place, three points behind us when the final table was put together. We scored 114 goals in thirty-nine First Division games, so the supporters got good value for money. There was plenty of entertainment along the way, as well as a good grounding for me in some of the finer details of management.

With funds tight, I only brought in one player that season. Willie Pettigrew, who had been a regular goal scorer for Jim at Dundee United as well as for Willie at Motherwell prior to that, was someone I thought would do a turn in the First Division. The fact he was at Hearts, managed by my old teammate Alex MacDonald, should have made it straightforward, but it didn't turn out that way. I approached Doddie about the possibility of taking Willie in on loan until the end of the season and he was happy with that proposition, so everything was in place. He had come in, played well and scored a few goals – then we drew St Mirren in the fifth round of the Scottish Cup and suddenly the goalposts changed. Wallace Mercer, the chairman at Tynecastle, must have seen the pound signs when he realised we had a big local derby coming up in the Cup and told Doddie that we could only keep Pettigrew if we stumped up £10,000. In a flash, any profit we stood to make from the St Mirren tie was winging its way to the Hearts bank account rather than our own. Alex's hands were tied, but I knew Willie would score goals so we agreed to pay the fee. To rub salt into the wounds, we lost the Cup game 4–3 at Love Street.

That result was a minor blip in what was a very good run, culminating with the presentation of the league trophy at Cappielow on the final day of the season after we had clinched the First Division prize. My old club Kilmarnock were the visitors and we served up another cracker of a game, running out 3–2 winners with a little help from some friends in high places. We'd be training on the pitch and knew it was rock hard, thanks to some good May weather. The groundsman had some pals at the local fire station and he called them out to flood the pitch with water and help us out – a hard bumpy pitch was no good for the type of team we had, they performed far better on a slicker surface. Fortunately we could call upon the local watch to turn it back in our favour. I'll never forget the television cameras coming down to film the occasion, panning out over a sun-soaked Clyde and then zooming in to puddles of water on the pitch. Fortunately nobody at the fire brigade HQ put two and two together!

A double from Dougie Robertson and a goal from John McNeil had edged us over the finishing line and more than 5,000 crammed into the ground to celebrate. The scenes at full-time were wonderful, with our fans in good voice and roaring their approval when Jim Duffy stepped forward to lift the trophy. They enjoyed their afternoon in the sun, that's for sure. I was treated to an unexpected dunk in the bath, fully clothed, at full-time as the players carried on the party back in the dressing room. We deserved to finish top of the league and it was good to see the squad letting their hair down after their sterling efforts over the course of the year.

Although the championship was obviously a priority, the work going on behind the scenes to strengthen the set-up was arguably just as significant. George Gillespie led the scouts at Morton and was one of the old school, working away and coming up with some excellent tips. Competing with the Old Firm on Clydeside was frustrating – there were quite a few local lads who slipped away when we were desperate to take them to

Morton. Stevie Fulton was the one that stands out. He was getting rave reviews as a schoolboy and we sat down with his parents to try and persuade them that Cappielow would be the best option, but he ended up at Celtic instead.

Still, we kept beavering away and looking to the future, a future that would be in the Premier Division. For the Morton supporters it was a case of taking their team back to where they belonged and it was fantastic to be able to do that for them. When the curtain fell on the 1983/84 season all of my attention was focused on the challenge ahead after winning promotion – but within days everything changed.

12

MANAGERIAL MERRY-GO-ROUND

While I celebrated winning the championship with Morton, the final day of the season brought its usual share of heartache for other managers and coaches up and down the land. Bobby Watson at Motherwell was among those going through the mill and as the champagne flowed at Cappielow to mark our promotion to the Premier Division he was tendering his resignation at Fir Park after his side's relegation from the top flight.

In the same Monday papers that were reporting on the events at Cappielow, there were stories tipping me to replace Bobby at Motherwell. It must have looked a bit bizarre from the outside, but there was logic to the train of thought that I'd be interested in swapping the chance of leading Morton into the new season for the opportunity of taking over at a struggling side that had just dropped through the trap door. For a start, the Morton board had made it clear that promotion didn't bring full-time football back to Cappielow. They had been down that route before and had their fingers burned financially, so caution was the order of the day. Meanwhile, Motherwell, despite falling into the First Division, were not going down the route of reverting to part-time status for their squad. That made it an attractive proposition for the next manager. On a more practical level, both myself and Tam Forsyth were based a short hop from Fir Park in Lanarkshire so there was an element of home comfort for us. Of course, none of that would have been relevant if the paper talk had been purely speculation. Other names had been mentioned in relation to the Motherwell job, including Eddie Hunter and Craig Brown, but we were being touted as the favourites.

There was a delay of a couple of weeks until Motherwell made their move, with Jock Brown in his capacity as a solicitor with Ballantyne and Copland doing the groundwork. The Motherwell chairman Ian Livingstone was a partner in the firm and Jock was the conduit between the club and I. We went on to have a long professional relationship, with Jock representing me in my various moves in later years. He has always had a very sharp legal brain and the fact that he also knows football inside out is obviously a real boon.

Jock is of course best known in the game as a commentator and for his time as general manager at Celtic, but he could play the game too. In fact, he'd be quick to tell you that he would have had a long and illustrious time in the sport had it not been for me – apparently it was during a schoolboy game in which he was tasked with marking me that he came to the conclusion he'd have to come up with a Plan B for his career path after I gave him the run around! He went on to study at Cambridge University and had been at the top of the legal profession in Scotland for decades – where did it all go wrong?!

As it happened, the solicitors at Motherwell's disposal weren't particularly challenged when it came to the negotiations to take me to Fir Park from Morton. I'd been working on a non-contract basis at Cappielow, with the agreement for me to manage the team through to the end of the season, so I was a free agent. There was no bad feeling between Morton and I; there had always been an understanding that if a full-time opportunity arose I would be keen to pursue it.

I was invited to Fir Park for an interview and was offered the job there and then. I didn't have to go away and think about it – I knew before I'd gone through the door on the way in that I would jump at the chance if they decided I was the man for the job. It meant at least another year in the First Division, but in the long run I felt Motherwell was a club with great potential to be a force again in the Premier Division. There had been some rough times and, like at Morton, the bank balance was not healthy, but I felt it was a gamble worth taking.

And it was a gamble. From the offset it was made clear that the finances were precarious, to say the least. The truth of the matter was that if we didn't get back to the Premier Division at the first attempt then full-time football would be a thing of the past and, more immediately, if we couldn't sell some of the more valuable playing assets for decent fees we might not stay afloat to see the season out. It was that serious. Maybe I was guilty of letting my ambition get the better of me, but I didn't doubt at any stage I could turn things around for Motherwell on and off the park. I also didn't doubt that it would be a difficult journey.

The debt sat at £750,000 and the banks were beginning to get nervous, it was bordering on bankruptcy. We needed to raise £100,000 before a ball had been kicked, taking precedence over any footballing concerns. Still, there was no point that I ever questioned my decision to make the move.

Naturally after the good times at Cappielow, I still had an eye on events at Morton. Having lost McLean junior, they put their faith in my big brother Willie to lead them in the new Premier Division season. Willie, who had made his mark in management with Motherwell and Ayr United, had spent a successful year in Cypriot football – leading Pezeporokos to the Cup final over there – but was ready to come home and it was an ideal job for him. The fact he had the inside track from me throughout the previous season, with regular calls back and forth between us to chew things over as we always had done, meant he was able to hit the ground running. For Willie the aim was consolidation in the big league, but it was a tall order with a part-time squad. He did his best to strengthen the team I had left behind, but even with reinforcements it was still a bridge too far. It proved to be a one-season stay in the Premier Division, despite Willie's best efforts.

As he focused on that league, I was getting to grips with my first full season as a manager and looking forward to another tilt at the First Division. The months I had spent at Cappielow had given me a good feel for what we were up against and what would be required to win us that all important promotion. Although they had been relegated, the squad that reported for duty on my first day at work with Motherwell was not lacking in quality or potential. The defender Graeme Forbes was a stalwart, Ally Mauchlen in midfield was a real talent and Andy Harrow was a forward that Alex Ferguson had previously signed for Aberdeen – as references go, that isn't a bad one to have on your CV. There were youngsters with their best days ahead of them too, with Tom Boyd playing in the centre of the defence under Bobby Watson and showing signs of his ability. Chris McCart and Jim Griffin were breaking through too and Gary McAllister was also making waves.

While I was content enough with the squad at my disposal, believing I could build their confidence and improve them as individuals and as a group, I knew I wouldn't be able to keep them together. There had to be sacrifices.

Stuart Rafferty was the first to go, sold to Dundee for £27,500 and giving them good service. Kenny Black was next, with Hearts paying £30,000 to take him to Tynecastle. The remaining

£40,000 of the £100,000 target was made up by bringing the wage bill down and cutting other costs. In contrast, the players coming in as replacements were either from the free transfer list or for nominal fees. Andy Walker from Baillieston in the junior ranks was one we paid for after Bobby Watson had done the legwork with that deal. Iain McDonald was brought in from Partick and Gregor Stevens from Rangers without a penny in fees. I did pay our Jim £5,000 to bring Derek Murray in from Dundee United, but that proved to be a bargain.

When you're shopping in that type of market there are always risks, and as it happened, Gregor and Iain didn't play too many games before I moved them on, preferring to concentrate my efforts on bringing through youngsters to fill the gaps in the squad. Producing home-grown players was clearly the best route forward for a club like Motherwell, where gates were never likely to support big transfer fees or high wages. The problem I quickly discovered was that the youth structure wasn't as productive as I thought it should have been. In theory it was the lifeblood of the club, but in practice it wasn't the case.

Aside from that, I was never comfortable with there being what was effectively a pub within the stadium. You could smell the drink as you came in the front door at Fir Park and I hated that. The social club eventually found a new home opposite the stadium, orchestrated by John Chapman, and that was something I had pushed for – I think it benefited the social club committee as well as us, as it gave them a new lease of life. The space under the stand was opened up for hospitality purposes so created a new revenue stream for the football club. Similarly, the squash complex the club had built in the late 1970s changed hands. Large sums of money had been invested in the hope of eventually turning a profit to be ploughed back into the football club, but instead it proved to be a financial burden and we cut our losses.

It was all part of the streamlining process to get things back on an even keel.

When I think back to the things I got involved in behind the scenes in those early days it is amazing there was time to fit it all in, but I had to make the time. It was all part of the process of building for the future.

On the football front, my efforts to get the youth development programme back on track gathered pace when I took over the Airdrie and Coatbridge arm of Nottingham Forest Boys' Club. Bobby Jenks and John Taggart were the coaches leading the club and they were doing a fine job. By linking up with them we opened up an instant network of talented local juvenile players. I went a stage further and appointed Bobby as a full-time scout, recognising his ability to pick out a player. He'd been doing similar work for Forest on a part-time basis but I felt he could be even more productive if he had the opportunity to join the staff. Bobby, who is now in his second stint at the club, was awarded a well-deserved testimonial in 2010 in recognition of forty years' service to youth football in Lanarkshire and had a big part to play in what we achieved at Motherwell.

We all worked round the clock to improve things. I was in during the day for training with the full-time players and catching up with admin in the office and then back at night to work with the part-timers we had on the books or taking in games left, right and centre. There were eight or nine players who were on part-time deals, with the likes of Crawford Baptie coming in from Falkirk and Raymond Blair from East Fife. It was a juggling act and a real test at times, but we had to keep the plates spinning.

Tam Forsyth had come in to work alongside me full-time, with Cammy Murray coaching on a part-time basis. We were a good team, all with different qualities but with a similar view on how we could achieve our aims. The interesting thing about Tam is that he is perceived as the big tough guy, going back to his playing days at Rangers. In actual fact, at Motherwell he was the good cop to my bad cop. It was Tam who the players would turn to and it was Tam who lifted the heads when I was being the hard taskmaster. You need that at every club and he did it brilliantly, it was a huge support to me.

Cammy Murray was a different kettle of fish completely. He would take the reserves – and it must have been the only club in the country where the players looked forward to playing in the second string, if only to listen to Cammy's tales. He was a wonderful storyteller and certainly kept things interesting. Much more than that, he had a terrific football brain and was a great help to me in terms of bouncing ideas around and thinking things through.

The fact the three of us gelled so quickly was very important. The first stage of the project facing us was getting out of the First Division at the earliest opportunity. My last game as Morton manager had been against Kilmarnock and the same opposition came through to Fir Park for my debut in the Motherwell dugout. It was the same outcome too – with full points again, although this time it was courtesy of a 2–0 win rather than the 3–2 I'd had with Morton.

It was an encouraging start but defeats in the next two games, in the league against Hamilton then the League Cup against Ayr, brought us back down to earth with a bump. The first half of the season was topsy-turvy, one step forward and one step back at times. There was a real sticky spell in the middle, where we lost four out of five in the First Division during a horrible run, but as we worked with the group over time it began to gel.

As we moved into 1985 we went ten games unbeaten, dropping just two points along the way, and by the end of that we had pushed our way up from sixth place in the table to the top. It looked like we'd timed our run perfectly and although we dropped back a place in the last month of the season, when Clydebank briefly replaced us in first place, we held our nerve in the final games to win the championship by two points. It was a sense of relief as much as joy when I realised we had done it. In many ways it is the biggest single achievement of my career because it saved a great football club from consequences that could have been catastrophic. It was win or bust, really.

I received the Manager of the Year award from the Scottish Football Writers' Association at their end of season dinner in Glasgow and it was maybe only at that point that I reflected on what it meant for me individually. Up to then it had been all about the end goal for Motherwell, about keeping the club afloat. The championship was a means to an end; promotion was the real prize.

Clydebank had chased us hard and held on to take the second promotion spot, with Falkirk and Hamilton in the pack behind them. When you consider there were clubs of the size of Partick, Ayr, Kilmarnock, St Johnstone and Airdrie all in that division you get an idea of how competitive it was. Premier Division football was what every one of those teams was striving for and it was cutthroat stuff at times, with so much at stake. We had to tread a fine line between instant results and long-term planning, but I was heartened by what I could see in the pipeline. Phillip O'Donnell, Chris McCart, Jim Griffin and Jamie Dolan were all showing great promise and from a football and business perspective it was heartening.

What we never disguised was the fact we were a selling club. Some people may see that as a lack of ambition, but to me it was a strength. We could sit down with young players and even their parents and really sell Motherwell to them as a club that would help them realise their potential. If they came to us, worked hard and made their mark then we would not stand in their way if the right opportunity came along.

The same principles applied to contract negotiations. We used the old 'Jim McLean' approach and got those with better potential on long-term deals, but those were always on the understanding that it was a means of providing us with some security as well as giving the players stability rather than trying to shackle people to us. Generally, players were happy with that.

It appealed to the right type of player – not those interested in short-term gain or an ego trip, but boys who could see the bigger picture and had faith in their ability to keep climbing the ladder. I always made a point of telling them you had to earn the right to play and then earn the right to get your big move. I was proud when they succeeded.

One of the first things I did after taking over was get Gary McAllister and Tam Boyd secured on improved but longer contracts. I didn't for a minute expect they would see them out as they were always likely to be in demand, but it meant we had a better bargaining position.

When I look at Fir Park as it stands now, I don't just see the steel and the bricks and mortar that make it what it is today. I see the faces of the players who made it possible. Andy Walker cost £1,000 to bring in from the juniors and was sold for £375,000 when he went to Celtic. Fraser Wishart cost the same when I took him in from Pollock juniors and was sold for £275,000 to St Mirren in 1989. Further down the line, Tom Boyd went for £800,000 to Chelsea and Phillip O'Donnell commanded a fee of £1.75 million when he earned his big move to Celtic in 1994. The millions of pounds that came in through transfer fees were a very clear indication that the policy we adopted right at the start of the journey was the right one for Motherwell Football Club.

MENORCA
GIN XORIGUER

MENORCA
GIN XORIGUER

TRIANGLE ▼POSTALS

5705.2 / foto:© Juanjo Pons
8424455507006 / D.L.B.:25874-2007

With my business hat on, I knew it was a solid strategy. With my manager's cap, it wasn't always easy to watch your best players heading for pastures new. That hit home at the end of our first season when, as anticipated, Gary McAllister was the subject of firm interest. Gary had been a star for us in midfield and when the time came for him to spread his wings I effectively acted as his agent. It started to gather pace when Gordon Milne, who was in charge at Leicester City, appeared one night at a Lanarkshire Cup tie against Hamilton. You got used to seeing scouts scattered around the stand, but Gordon was standing away on the far side at Douglas Park, obviously having a quiet look. As soon as I saw him I had a good idea who he was watching over. Gordon asked me to meet him at the airport hotel in Glasgow after that match and it turned out he was interested in a couple of our players – and thankfully not expecting to get two for the price of one, even though he knew that we were strapped for cash. He offered £250,000 for Gary and Ally Mauchlen, split £150,000 and £100,000 respectively. It was an era where managers could do deals man to man, without agents caught in the middle, and both players were happy for me to look after their interests as best I could. Of course, they had the final say and the power to do as they wished, but it was a mark of the trust they had in me.

I made sure Gordon looked after them and also pushed for the signing fees to be structured differently. Ally was older and had family commitments, so having the fee paid upfront was beneficial to him. With Gary, I asked that the lump sum was spread over the duration of his contract because for younger players I never felt comfortable with money being showered on them. As it happened, Gary was a huge success and quickly had a new and improved contract in place, but nobody would grudge him that. As I said before, if you earn your move and fulfil your potential the rewards tend to follow.

For those two the road to England was one that allowed them to better themselves, but from a football perspective it could have been devastating for us as a team. We'd won promotion then had the feet kicked from beneath us, with the championship-winning midfield snatched away in one fell swoop. But as we did so often along the way, all we could do was go back to the drawing board and concentrate on filling those gaps and trying to keep the momentum we had started to build with the run of results in the First Division. It was still a work in progress, getting a feel for the players and the characters we had in the dressing room. Andy Walker was a good example, a player who we spent time with to make the most of the attributes he had.

Andy had been recruited as a left-winger and started out playing in that position for us. What struck me straight away was that he didn't have the pace to be a wide man, but he was blessed with speed of thought. I moved him forward to play as a second striker, off the front, where he could put his creativity to use and find spaces to play in rather than being head-to-head with a full-back as he had been. Andy took to it like a duck to water and also showed a nose for goal, to the point that in time he was moved forward to play as the main striker. I'm certain he wouldn't have played for Celtic had it not been for that change in emphasis. Andy didn't have a bag of tricks and he wasn't the best crosser of a ball, but he could take it in to the feet comfortably and was a good finisher, both aspects that became trademarks of his game.

What you have to do is watch every player in 'their' position and take time to gather your thoughts. There's no sense in writing anyone off without looking for another way to maximise their potential. Phillip O'Donnell was a left-back and a central defender before we settled on him in the midfield, where he proved to be a natural. Tam Boyd also played in the centre of the defence before he became recognised as a full-back, although of course he returned to his old stomping ground in the middle of the back line with Celtic in his twilight years. Those three examples are notable but in reality all of them had enough natural talent to make a difference wherever they played.

In some cases it was a very different proposition. If I couldn't find a slot for some players, I would try them in various positions as a last throw of the dice. I had to find a position that worked for them and for the team rather than show them the door. When you have no money in the pot for transfers, you have little option but to experiment and make the best of the resources at your disposal. I tried different things until I found a position that worked, not always because I was confident it would pay off but often because there was no other choice.

Transfer activity consisted of wheeling and dealing in those early days, although the board were as supportive as they could be. Director John Chapman was a great support. He knew the type of character I was and was receptive to what I wanted to do.

One of the only issues I had at that level was with the leaking of stories to the press, particularly when it came to transfers. It may have seemed like a minor issue, but it actually had the potential to cause serious grief. All it took was word of my interest in a particular player to get out in the public domain and other clubs were alerted, so there was competition that we wouldn't otherwise have had for their signature and also the potential for the asking price to be pushed up as a consequence. Quite simply, we couldn't afford that – the budget was tiny in the first place.

Unfortunately not everyone within the club could see the damage the leaks could cause. I was pretty sure where the information was passing through, but proving it was more difficult. Everyone on the board had their own roles and responsibilities, with John Chapman the financial figurehead. John, a butcher by trade, was a prudent operator and a shrewd man; eventually he said to me not to flag up potential signings to the board to avoid any temptation for news to leak out, and just to go straight to him. He had the power to give me a 'yes' or a 'no' when it came to what was left in the pot for new recruits. With just the two of us in the loop, it ensured confidentiality and solved that particular problem.

It didn't make any difference to the other difficulty I had when it came to dealing with the board – that was John's ruthless approach to money. Every single penny was a prisoner where he was involved and the familiar phrase whenever I asked for money for a player, no matter how much or how little was involved, was, 'You can work on it.' Whoever it was, he wanted them for less. I can only ever remember one exception to that rule, but I'll touch on that later. Otherwise, it was always a case of asking me to go away and try and haggle that little bit more. I became a past master at negotiating cut-price deals, all because of John's insistence on keeping a tight hold on the purse strings. Although it frustrated me at times, we actually made a good team because I always liked to look after the business as well as the football team. I was never a manager who believed in separating the two sides of the club or in breaking the bank to gamble on success. The books always had to balance during that period in the history of Motherwell and the records show we managed to do that while delivering success on the park at the same time, something that I'm very proud of.

The first stage of that was that First Division Championship in 1985/86. The next was keeping our place in the Premier Division, but we needed a helping hand along the way. We always needed to strengthen to prepare for the Premier Division, but after losing McAllister and Mauchlen, that need was even more pressing.

The sale of those two to Leicester had given a little bit of room for manoeuvre, but not as much as we realistically needed to be comfortable in the top flight.

I turned to Dundee United for my biggest signing of the summer, bringing in John Reilly for £50,000. He had been part of the championship-winning squad at Tannadice just two years earlier so had been over the course at that level before. John unfortunately had his time with us cut short when he suffered a horrendous Achilles injury. We all thought he had been lost to the game, but fortunately advances in surgery allowed John to make a return in later years.

Jim Weir, a midfielder I knew from his time with Partick, was brought in for a £20,000 fee. Jim had been out in Germany playing with Kassell in the Second Division for four years, but was looking to get back home. After the experience he had on the continent it had the hallmarks of a sound move, but bad luck with injury was again a factor and he moved on to Cumnock in the juniors after a season. Brian Wright, another midfielder, came in from Hamilton Accies for £20,000 and played a big part for us over the next couple of years while we also pushed a few more of the young players into the first-team fold and recruited Jim Clark from Kilmarnock. None were blockbuster deals by any stretch of the imagination and it was always going to be a case of doing our best to keep up with the pace in that first season back in the Premier Division.

We opened up with a 0–0 draw against Clydebank before two difficult trips to face Celtic and then Aberdeen. We lost 2–1 at Parkhead but came away from Pittodrie with a point after that game ended 1–1, enough to keep us hovering above the relegation places. Unfortunately we couldn't sustain that points average and went on a really tough run that brought just a couple of wins in the next ten games and left us bottom of the table. We rallied in the second half of the season – beating Rangers, Dundee United and Hibs in the space of four games – and managed to overtake Clydebank. But ninth was as good as it got for us.

That is when the good fortune you sometimes need in football came into play. Just when it looked like all was lost, the old chestnut of league reconstruction reared its head. It just goes to show how many years we have been going round in circles, but in the spring of 1986 the familiar debate about the best set-up was raging on. We had a ten-team top division but had various options for change on the table. Eventually, after the usual protracted discussions, the vote was taken to expand the Premier Division to twelve teams.

At one stage a breakaway was being threatened by nine of the teams in the top league, but in the end a compromise was reached with a 12-12-14 set-up agreed by the thirty-eight senior clubs. Crucially from a selfish point of view, it meant no relegation that season and two teams from the First Division winning promotion as usual. Both Clydebank and my own Motherwell team were saved from the drop.

From the outside it might seem like a hollow victory, but with so much riding on maintaining top-level football at Fir Park, there were no arguments from us. Nobody was satisfied with the results that season – there obviously needed to be improvement – but we had been given a second chance to get it right. I was determined we would make the most of it.

13

RED ALERT

There can't be many professions in the world like football management. Within the space of a few months I went from fearing for my own job to being offered the chance to take on what was arguably the biggest task in the country at that time. It was the winter of 1986. I'd come through the experience of avoiding relegation the previous season, when I knew my neck was on the line at Motherwell. Ultimately it is a results-driven business and whether I'd won the First Division Championship or not, the performances back in the Premier Division had not been what I or the directors expected.

Fortunately the board held their nerve and kept faith in me and my long-term vision for the club. They backed my judgement as the squad went through the next stage of the rebuilding, with nine new faces added for the 1986/87 season, and gave me the time and space I needed to make my mark. By my reckoning, it takes three seasons for any manager to truly put their own stamp on a club and this was my third campaign. It was judgement time.

In contrast to the struggles of the previous year, we hit the ground running in the 1986/87 season. We lost once in the first five games, against Celtic, and went on a run to the semi-final of the League Cup. Again Celtic were our downfall, beating us on penalties. That early form set us up for a consistent campaign, where we sat comfortably mid-table throughout. It was steady progress, which was exactly what I had been promising the directors. What I hadn't bargained for was the call I received in November 1986. It came from Dick Donald, chairman of Aberdeen. After all of the success at home and abroad, Alex Ferguson had announced his intention to accept Manchester United's invitation to become their new manager. It left a huge void at Pittodrie and they had decided that I could fill it. I believe Alex may have recommended me for the job, but as was normally the case, it was the sports writer Jim Rodger who was in the thick of it all. He seemed to know more about what was going on than I did, so many people confided in him.

It was arranged for me to travel through to Perth to meet with Dick and his son Ian, who would go on to succeed him as chairman. We met at the Station Hotel in the middle of town and they didn't waste any time in offering me the job or trying to persuade me it was the right move at that stage in my career. They were certainly willing to back up their argument with cash, promising me a £20,000 pay rise without blinking. How on earth they knew what my Motherwell salary was I'll never know, but again I have a hunch Mr Rodger was involved.

The Donalds asked me to go away and think about their offer overnight, an offer which included the prospect of serious investment in the playing squad if that was what I felt was required. The only stipulation from their side was that I retained Teddy Scott as part of the backroom team. Teddy, a legend at Pittodrie for the incredible service he gave them during his lifetime, was a huge loss to football when he passed away in 2012. I would have had absolutely no issue with keeping him on my staff, his experience and knowledge would have been a huge asset. It certainly had been to Fergie, who had even taken Teddy

Early days: That's me, second from left in the front row, with my Larkhall Academy teammates in 1961. Jim Kirkland (third from right, back row), Billy Dickson (second from right, back row) and George Russell (back left) all went on to play at the top level.

Big break: A handshake with Willie Waddell seals my step up into the professional game with Kilmarnock in 1963.

Champions: The league title-winning Kilmarnock squad, with me third from the left in the front row, deserves its place in Rugby Park folklore.

Earning my stripes: I went from boy to man as a Kilmarnock player; in this picture I'm taking on the experienced Motherwell man Joe Wark.

National service:
Displaying my collection
of Scotland jerseys
during my time in the
international fold.

Mother's pride: My
mum, seen here with
me and my brothers Jim
(right) and Willie, was a
huge influence on all of
our lives and careers.

The Killie squad
and me (far left)
taking time out
for some rest and
relaxation at the
Seamill Hydro.

Big decision: This is one of the pictures of Beth and I that appeared in the newspapers when we decided to turn down the opportunity to move to London when Chelsea came calling.

African adventure: On the ball during a kick-about with youngsters during Kilmarnock's trip to Rhodesia in 1970, a tour that made quite a few headlines at the time.

Perfect match: Beth and I on our wedding day in 1970 with my teammates Jim Cook, Ross Mathie, Billy Dickson, John Gilmour and Andy King.

Jumping for joy: Celebrating Sandy Jardine's goal in our European Cup Winners' Cup semi-final victory against Bayern Munich at Ibrox.

Derby delight: This goal against Celtic put us on our way to a 3-0 victory in the New Year's Day game in 1975.

Special collection: My amateur and senior international caps, my medals, the jersey I wore in the European Cup Winners' Cup final in 1972 as well as the No.10 shirt I swapped with my hero Ferenc Puskas when I played against Real Madrid for Kilmarnock. On the right is the shirt put together for the Glasgow select team to wear in a Silver Jubilee celebration in 1977 – blue for Rangers, green for Celtic, red and yellow for Partick Thistle and there were black and white cuffs to represent Queen's Park.

Royal approval: That's me meeting the Queen ahead of that Silver Jubilee fixture in 1977, resplendent in that special kit.

Learning my trade: This is the Class of '83 at the SFA coaching course in Largs, with me in the centre of the front row. Also among the familiar faces are Jock Stein, Billy Bingham and the German coach Karl-Heinz Heddergott. And among the 'pupils' are a youthful-looking Craig Brown, Alex Smith, John Lambie, my Rangers colleague Alex Miller and many others who went on to become friends and rivals in the years that followed.

Winning formula: The Morton team and I with the First Division trophy we won during my first season in management.

Silk and steel: The Motherwell squad assembled for the run to the Scottish Cup final in 1991, one of the most satisfying seasons of my career.

Happy memories: My mother and father were all smiles as they looked forward to Jim and I leading our teams out in the Scottish Cup final at Hampden in 1991.

Mixed emotions: This picture of Stevie Kirk and I displaying the Scottish Cup on the Hampden track is one of the few taken of me after the final whistle, after I was coaxed out of the dressing room during the celebrations.

Warm welcome: The reception we received at Fir Park on the evening of the Cup final was incredible and it showed how much the Cup win meant to the Motherwell supporters.

Pride and joy: Beth and I with our beautiful baby Lorna, whose birth was by far the biggest and happiest occasion in our life together.

VIP invitation: Little Lorna makes herself at home as Beth and I show her around the Fir Park boardroom.

Fresh challenge: I'm joined by my family on the day my appointment as Dundee United manager was confirmed in 1996.

Toasting a hat-trick: Three consecutive Bell's Manager of the Month awards during my first season at Tannadice demonstrated the success we had as a team during that period.

Family life: My daughter Lorna and her beloved Yorkshire Terrier, Ellie.

with him to the World Cup as part of the Scotland coaching team for the finals in Mexico earlier that year.

I drove back up the road with my head in a bit of a spin. It wasn't every day that you received that type of opportunity. Bearing in mind it was only three years after Aberdeen had won the European Cup Winners' Cup and European Super Cup, they were still very much in the spotlight – and not just in Scotland. It was, quite simply, a huge chance for me to go to one of the leading lights of that time.

I arrived back in Motherwell and had a restless night. That morning I called John Chapman and asked him to come and meet me at the office, which was in a little house next to the stadium. I told him about the offer from Aberdeen, but if I'd been expecting John to jump in and try to match them with a wage increase, I was mistaken. As usual, he soaked it all in and didn't budge. The ball was in my court, but Motherwell wouldn't be getting involved in an auction.

There was only one thing to do. I phoned Aberdeen to thank them for their interest – and politely declined. I look back on that moment and consider it to be probably the biggest decision I have ever made in football. I can say, hand on heart, that not once have I regretted it. Whoever followed Alex Ferguson at Pittodrie faced an impossible task. He would be the first to admit that what he achieved in the years building up to that point was impossible to repeat. What I was pleased about was the fact the whole situation remained private. Nobody within the circle involved, including Jim Rodger, broke the confidence that I had asked for and not a word was mentioned in the press. I didn't want to draw attention to myself and I also didn't like the idea of anyone else feeling like they were second choice.

When the appointment eventually came, the choice was a surprise one. Ian Porterfield was brought in from south of the border and, as I had feared, he found it a very difficult assignment. Comparisons with Fergie were inevitable and it didn't work out for Ian. It was unfair on him because the team was in a period of transition, with many of the players who had done so well in the first half of the 1980s naturally beginning to wind down. Alex Smith, next in line, enjoyed greater success but still found to his cost that the expectations remained sky high because of the glory years. Nobody could have lived up the demands, as even Willie Miller discovered when he took charge.

The football concerns were the primary reason for my decision to reject the offer from Aberdeen, but I had other considerations. My mother and father lived near to our home in Ashgill and were at an age where I wanted to be close, so relocating would have been a wrench. On an even more practical level, the house prices in Aberdeen at the height of the oil boom were eye-watering and even with the prospect of a big wage hike I wasn't convinced it equated to a good deal in the face of the rise in living costs. All in all, the signs told me to stick, not twist.

On top of all of that, I had a loyalty to Motherwell and to the players I had brought to the club. There had been a bit of a whirlwind in the transfer market just a few months earlier as we prepared for our second season in the Premier Division and it wouldn't have been fair on the players I had brought in for me just to clear my desk and move to Aberdeen. I had sold them my plan for the future at Motherwell and they had all bought in to that. It was right that I stayed and finished the job that I had started.

The second half of 1986 was pivotal in everything that followed for me at Fir Park. Some of the signings I completed in that period were among the best I ever made. Dougie Arnott, spotted playing for Pollok in the juniors, was a key one. He cost all of £1,500 but in reality was worth a million dollars, a real star for me. Dougie, a Carluke boy, had played in the Scottish Junior Cup final at Fir Park a couple of years earlier but I'm glad we managed to make sure he had plenty more opportunities to perform on that pitch. Stevie Kirk cost a bit more, in the region of £20,000, when he came in from East Fife around a year earlier, but, again, he repaid that several times over. I tried a few times for Stevie before we eventually struck a deal, but there was no way I was going to give up. He was just twenty-two when he signed and his best years were at Fir Park.

Others who arrived with us in that period of consolidation in the Premier Division included Craig Paterson and Tom McAdam from Rangers and Celtic respectively, Paul Smith from Dunfermline, Gordon Mair from Lincoln City and John Philliben from Doncaster Rovers. John had been a European Youth Championship winner with Scotland just a few years earlier and we got him at a time when he was ready to shine. We were starting to cast the net wider to build and improve, with a mix of youth and experience, and I could see a team coming together that could compete in the Premier Division for years to come.

Throughout that time I could rely on the support of my big brothers – I was constantly on the phone to Willie and Jim, bouncing ideas around and leaning on their experience. The only time that changed was when we played against one another. Then we would agree football talk was off limits for the week, even though I'd actually go and stay with Jim on the eve of games in Dundee when we were facing each other when I was a player. Once we stepped out on the pitch we were always completely professional and committed to winning, regardless of what it meant for our brothers.

I can remember when Willie was in charge with Motherwell, I was part of the Rangers team that faced them in the Scottish Cup semi-final in 1976. From being two goals behind, we went on to win 3–2 and knocked them out. It was Willie's last real chance of success as a manager, but I had to put that out of my mind and concentrate on my team. It is difficult to take pleasure from winning in that situation, because you know how much your brother is hurting, but it was just part and parcel of our life together in the game.

I looked forward to the calls on a Sunday to talk over the weekend's events. Jim's fiery outbursts became legendary, while Willie was a bit more reserved. Me? I would say I was somewhere in the middle. I could have my moments, but I don't think anyone could match Jim for volatility when he felt he had suffered an injustice. But no matter how intense the rivalry was, we never let football get in the way. We were brothers first and foremost, players and managers second.

In time I worked alongside Willie, when he returned to Fir Park as part of the community coaching team that was so vital to our attempts to become central to life in the town and surrounding area. Willie also helped in other ways, lending his expertise on match days by watching from the stands and reporting back at half-time to help me shape things and adjust as necessary. It was fantastic to have his knowledge at my disposal and he had an important part to play. All of that was running in tandem with the main aim of improving the team, although progress at times was slower than I would have liked, as the restrictions on spending made it a marathon rather than a sprint.

We finished eighth in the 1986/87 season and held that position the following year, dropping a place to ninth in 1988/89. We were solid but unspectacular, and it would take something, or someone, spectacular to change that.

14

MEMORIES OF A LEGEND

They say one player can't make a team, and I agree. But what an individual can do is change the mindset of every other person around him, and in Davie Cooper we were lucky enough to have that man at Motherwell. The signing of Coop in the summer of 1989 was a turning point for us. We went from a team battling to survive in the Premier Division to one that went into every single match believing we could win. That was the magnitude of the impact he had at Fir Park. I, like tens of thousands of others, will forever be grateful for that all too short time.

Had it not been for Davie's tragic death, he would have gone on to have succeeded me as Motherwell manager if I'd had my way. In my mind he was perfect for the role and I would have loved to have seen what he could have achieved. Unfortunately we'll never know, but in my heart of hearts I know he could have been as successful as a manager as he was as a player – and that is praise indeed.

I look back on many signings with fond memories for different reasons, whether young players like Phillip O'Donnell and Tam Boyd, who went on to great things, or loyal and trusted servants like Stevie Kirk, who did me proud. But when it comes to the pound for pound best piece of business I ever did, I have to say the recruitment of Davie Cooper for Motherwell has to be at the top of the list.

Where did the inspiration come from? It was, I have to admit, from the gents toilets of an Italian restaurant in Crossford. It was there that I had the conversation that changed everything for me as a manager and for Motherwell. Beth and I would regularly go out for a Saturday evening meal with three other couples. Tam Forsyth and Davie Cooper would join us with their wives, as well as Coop's good friend Ricky Jordan and his wife.

It was a throwaway line from Ricky in the gents that planted the seed. Ricky mentioned how disillusioned Coop was with life at Rangers under Graeme Souness. I said it would be a dream if we could attract him to Motherwell, not for a minute thinking it was possible. Ricky's response was, 'I don't think it's out of the question.' We went back to the table, my mind racing, and not another word about it was uttered. Conversation was never really focused on the day job, so it wasn't a subject that would have cropped up. Certainly Davie would never have brought it up and it wasn't something I would have been comfortable discussing with him for fear of being accused of tapping him up. Instead I waited until Monday morning, as long a thirty-six hours in football as I've spent, and got straight on the line to Ibrox to speak to Walter Smith. Poor Walter probably hadn't had time to get his coat off before the phone was ringing, but I didn't want to let the dust settle. I told him that I'd heard on the grapevine that Coop was unhappy, that he wanted to play more regular football. Walter was adamant that it was the first he knew about it and from my point of view it didn't sound promising, certainly not as though they had already thought about moving him on.

Wattie asked me to leave it with him, but I was already feeling deflated. The only fortunate thing was I hadn't mentioned anything about it to Coop, so I wouldn't have to explain myself to him. Then I got a call back from Walter. They were prepared to come to an agreement to do Davie a turn, given the length of service he had given the club. I didn't know whether to laugh or cry, I was that excited about it all.

There were still major hurdles to overcome, firstly in getting hold of the funds to make it happen and secondly in persuading him that his future lay at Fir Park. The first of those proved far easier than I had anticipated. I went to John Chapman, as I did for every signing, expecting to have a battle on my hands. I told him I needed £50,000 to sign Davie Cooper, and for the first time ever, and the last, he replied, 'I'd pay more than that to sign him.' There was no haggling. Rangers asked for £50,000 and we paid it. I believe they looked after Davie as part of the agreement, recognising his loyalty to the club over the course.

When it came to convincing Coop, again I expected at least a bit of work. But there wasn't a bit of it. When I went to him and told him we'd reached an agreement with Rangers, he didn't need to think twice, even with a tighter wage structure than he was used to. He saw it as a new challenge and knew how much I valued him, not just for his ability on the pitch but for the influence he could have off the park. The bottom line was he just wanted to play – that was his motivation and that's the best there can be.

He was quite clearly an individual player of the highest quality, but it was his attitude that was just as critical for Motherwell as a club. Where prior to his arrival we would go to Parkhead or Ibrox and try to steal a point, with Coop in the side we ran out at those grounds with a determination to go all out for victory. He didn't fear anyone or any team, sometimes to the point that I had to try to reel him in a bit. I used to talk to him before those big games, particularly against Celtic, and tell him that the opposition booing and jeering him was a mark of their respect. But at the same time, I asked him not to antagonise them and just to let it wash over him. What did he do? He would go straight out and start stretching and warming up in front of the Celtic fans in the Jungle, lapping it up as they bayed for him. He thrived on that type of situation, always expecting to have the last laugh.

While in public I tried to temper that type of thing, deep down I could see the impact it had on the players around him and particularly the younger ones like Tam Boyd and Phillip O'Donnell. All of a sudden they saw there was a way to take on the big boys and play them at their own game. They went on to another level when they had spent time training and playing alongside a master of his craft. Everyone at the club loved Davie and I have to dispel some of the myths surrounding the man the media labelled 'Moody Blue'. It is fair to say he didn't suffer fools gladly, but Davie had a real dry wit and was a hugely popular guy in the dressing room.

As for the suggestion he was lazy, something that had been levelled at him from time to time, I have to say that too is wide of the mark. If you gave him a day off and asked what he'd spent his time doing, then nine times out of ten you discovered he'd been out for a run. He looked after himself and took a real pride in his profession. He was also a shrewd man, and had already started establishing himself with some media work. He was doing some television appearances and had the right type of unflappable nature for that.

He may have talked a good game, but I far preferred to watch him play it. His performances after joining us were exceptional and within a couple of months he was off to the Scotland squad by Andy Roxburgh for a World Cup qualifier against Norway. He had been out of the international picture for a couple of years at that point and wasn't sure about going back in, thinking it was maybe time to move aside and let the younger players have their chance. I talked him out of that, telling him to think how proud it made his old father to see him in a Scotland shirt. He saw sense and went on to win a couple of caps during his time with us, starting with that game against Norway and proving he could certainly still cut it at that level. If anything, with age and maturity he was better suited to international football than he had ever been.

He had so much to give on every level and I was desperate to get him involved on the training field. The problem was that he hated the word 'coaching'. Instead I asked him to play in reserve matches and help the young boys along and got Cammy Murray to involve Davie as much as possible with the training. I'd say, 'That thing you just did, go and show the boys how you do that.' Quick as a flash he'd hit back with, 'I'm not coaching.' I told him to forget coaching. Instead, look at it as teaching – there's a difference!

Although he had left Motherwell at the time of his death in 1995 and I had moved on to Hearts, my long-term plan if I had remained at Fir Park was to bring him back as part of the coaching staff – even if he would have hated that job title – with a view to him taking over as manager. I knew he would have rebelled against the very idea of moving into management if I had suggested it, so I thought I'd have to do it subtly. It was one of those ones that I felt I had to make it feel as though it was his own idea, to plant a few seeds and hope it grew from there. I just never got the chance to carry it through and that is football's loss. I'm thankful we at least had the opportunity to play him in a Motherwell shirt. What he did in that time was nothing short of remarkable. Graeme Souness had brought in Mark Walters and other big-money signings to play on the wing, but I wouldn't have swapped Davie for any of them.

We didn't want him to track back or to be covering every blade of grass. The idea was to get him on the ball as often as possible and let him conduct the game, which is exactly what he did. Of course, he would have been wasted without a target and in Stevie Kirk he had that, with the two of them striking up a great understanding. Coop also needed runners to enable him to mix things up, with Phillip O'Donnell and Tam Boyd having the engines to get past him and into the gaps. They always had wanted to do that, the difference once they were playing alongside Davie was that nine times out of ten he would pick a pass that found them in that space. It gave Tam and Phillip a new purpose and a new belief, bringing them on in leaps and bounds.

It was a sad day when he left Fir Park for the last time, moving on to Clydebank in 1994. He was going back to his first club, but it wasn't about sentimentality. It was just his burning desire to stay playing first-team football for as long as he could, even if that meant dropping down a level. He never lost his enthusiasm or love of the game. He was the same in that respect as he was when I first clapped eyes on him as a kid coming in the door at Ibrox in the 1970s.

He played against my Hearts side for the Bankies in a Scottish Cup tie on 7 February 1995. It proved to be the last time I saw him, little realising at the time that I'd never have the pleasure of watching him at work again. Within a matter of weeks, he had been struck down.

The day he collapsed will live with me forever. I was at Hearts by that point and was in the office when I got a call from Christine, Davie's wife. They were separated at that stage but she was beside herself with worry when she got through to me, trying to find out if I knew what was happening. It turned out she had heard on the radio that he had collapsed, but other than that she was in the dark.

So was I, with the news not filtering through to me by that point. I got on the phone and rang round, trying to get hold of Ricky Jordan in particular. His mobile was off, but eventually he rang me back from the car park of the Southern General Hospital, where he had gone to be by his friend's bedside. He confirmed what was already breaking on the radio and television that Davie had collapsed while filming a football coaching video with Charlie Nicholas at Broadwood. What wasn't public at that stage was that Davie was brain dead. Ricky was crying his eyes out as he explained to me just how terrible the situation was. There would be no recovery – it was as horribly simple as that.

The reaction to his death, heartfelt and genuine grief through-out the football community and beyond, did not surprise me. People united in their shock but also in their appreciation of one of the most naturally gifted football players ever to grace Scottish soil. He stood out a mile from the outset. As soon as I saw him at close quarters on the training pitch at Rangers I knew we had a star in the making. Crucially for an Old Firm player, he also couldn't be bullied or intimidated. I remember Roy Aitken trying to do that, but he soon found out that Davie was up for the battle. He protected the ball so well when he had to and could go past defenders like they weren't there when the opportunity presented itself.

My one regret I have is that I wasn't able to accept the invitation by Davie's brother, John, to give a reading at the funeral service. Quite simply, I wasn't strong enough to stand up and do that. It was still so raw and I was terribly cut up. Coop was a straightforward guy, never frightened to give an opinion, and usually it was a valid one. I hit it off with him from his first day at Rangers and the friendship built from there. My memories of the man and the footballer are glowing.

15

UNITED IN GRIEF

The death of Davie Cooper, such an important and influential character in the history of Motherwell Football Club, was a hammer blow to those who had worked alongside him. What none of us could possibly have predicted was that the grief we shared at that terrible time would become a horribly familiar emotion in the years that followed. I still struggle to make sense of the loss of Coop, Phillip O'Donnell, Jamie Dolan and Paul McGrillen, four young men, four wonderful individuals, and the passing of each left a huge void in the lives of so many people they touched during their time on this earth.

When we gathered together for Davie's funeral there was a sense of togetherness for those who had been with him on the incredible journey that culminated in the Scottish Cup final in 1991. The service should have marked the start of the healing process, but instead it was just the start of a nightmare period. I was driving home from a game at Falkirk when I first heard a radio report about Phillip's collapse during Motherwell's game against Dundee United at Fir Park in December 2007. Initially details were scarce and I frantically began calling round to try and find out more. Chris McCart, someone who had traditionally been a figurehead for the group of young players who had come through together, including Phillip, was the one who was able to confirm the gravity of the situation. It had quickly become clear that Phillip had passed away. I was absolutely shattered. It was a surreal experience. I had faced the situation following Davie's collapse so should have had a handle on the incredible mix of emotions that were swirling around. But I didn't. Nothing prepares you for news like that.

As a coach or manager you feel a responsibility to all of the players who fall under your wing, particularly those who have been with you man and boy. Phillip was one of those who I had watched come through the system and had tremendous respect for, a model pupil. Of course, it is easy to feel sorry for yourself in times of loss, but it was impossible to lose sight of those who suffered most. Phillip left behind his wife, Eileen, and four children who lost their husband and father far, far too soon. He and Eileen had been childhood sweethearts, having met at school, and I was at their wedding. They were perfect together.

When I went to visit Eileen to pay my respects, I felt hopelessly inadequate. There are no words you can find, no real comfort you can offer in a situation like that. I only hope the family took some solace from the total admiration I and so many others had for Phillip.

What made his death so hard to comprehend was the fact that Phillip was such an athlete. He had suffered from injury problems, mainly muscular, whilst with Celtic and Sheffield Wednesday but had gone back to Motherwell, initially to play under Terry Butcher in 2004, and was back on top form. The niggles were behind him and he was proving himself all over again. He was an experienced head by then, but still had the stamina to get up and down the pitch like he always had done. That was one of the strengths of his game from his earliest days in the Motherwell team, the ability to make surging runs and get past the opposition defenders. The fact he had been taken from us due to a medical condition just went to prove that nobody can take anything for granted. He had spent his life looking after himself and working hard, a consummate professional, but that offered no protection. It was so cruel.

The world's a worse place without Phillip, who was one of life's gentlemen. He came from a lovely family and was the baby of the household, the youngest of the children. His parents and his brother and sisters just doted on him. I actually got to know his family well through illness in our own family, with Phillip's brother-in-law Eddie Smith in hospital at Stonehouse at the same time as my father was. They were in neighbouring beds and, with Eddie being a former referee, the conversation on the ward invariably turned to football. We'd all have a good blether together at visiting time. With such a great support network around him, it was no surprise that Phillip had turned out the way he had. I can still remember him turning up at our house in Ashgill after our Lorna had been born, bringing a gift to congratulate us. He was always thinking of others.

I'm still in touch with his dad now and although time is supposed to be a healer, I don't think any of us will truly get over what happened, but we'll never forget him either. Phillip was the type of boy a father would be happy to have their daughter bring home to meet them, real son-in-law material. Reliable, considerate and an all-round nice guy. I still wince when I think back to his debut, when I actually tore a strip off him for being just too nice. We played against St Mirren and I had pitched our rookie in at left-back, which wasn't his position at all. But he didn't complain, he got on with the job in hand. Unfortunately he was up against Kenny McDowell that day and Kenny, as an experienced campaigner, obviously thought he could play on Phillip's inexperience. He started to rough him up, giving him a real torrid time. It was like a wee boy being knocked around, and I was livid. I suppose the easiest thing would have been to have taken him off, but instead of doing that I got right in his face at half-time and told him he'd have to stand up for himself. I know many young players who would have disappeared into their shell, never to be seen again, but not Phillip. He rolled up his sleeves and took me at my word, toughening up and giving a good account of himself. And so a star was born. He never really looked back.

Nobody was happier than me to see Phillip back enjoying his football again and the fact he was wearing Motherwell colours was a bonus. He had his moves to Celtic and to England, but it was time for him to come home. After his death I thought the club and Mark McGhee, as manager at the time, handled the situation magnificently. They were dignified, respectful and showed real leadership when it was needed more than ever before. I think the overwhelming feeling at that time was one of astonishment. For any player to die on the pitch is horrific, not least for those who were at the game and witnessed the tragedy unfold.

Unfortunately collapses and heart problems have become an all too frequent feature of football and I applaud the efforts being made to improve detection and prevention procedures. Dr Stuart Hillis of the SFA is an eminent cardiologist and clearly has the expertise to drive things forward whilst clubs are also taking on far more of a responsibility for monitoring. There is no saying anyone could have done anything to prevent Phillip's death, but if improvements can help in any way, no matter how small, then we have to embrace them.

There was a certain irony that Phillip's finest hour, his Scottish Cup final goal, came against Dundee United, the same team he faced in his last game. The two sets of supporters united in their grief following that tragic game; in fact, the whole of football came together. Fir Park became like a shrine as people tried in their own way to come to terms with what had happened. I never heard anyone with a bad word to say about Phillip, which in football must be unique. He was never criticised and although underrated as a player, in my opinion, was respected throughout the game.

While we were still reeling from the loss of Coop and Phillip, we suffered another sickener when news of Jamie Dolan's death broke in August 2008. I was overseas at the time, coaching with Ross Mathie and his Scotland youth squad at the Nordic Cup, so felt terribly isolated from what was going on back home. Jamie had been out jogging, getting himself in shape for an indoor masters tournament, when he suffered a heart attack. He was just thirty-nine, just a young man who should have had many years in front of him. He was another one of my boys at Motherwell, one who had come through the ranks and who I felt a particular responsibility for. Jamie had lost his father at an early age and become a dad when he was still young after marrying his childhood sweetheart, Elaine, so he had a lot of responsibility on his shoulders. Because of that I tried to be an influence on his life and his career and I hope I did a good job in that respect. It was heartbreaking to see Jamie's own son, Dean, end up losing his dad so early in his own life.

Jamie was a quiet and unassuming type of man, but on the pitch he was a real player's player. He was the ball winner, the one who was willing to knuckle down and do the hard graft. Selfless. Jamie came to the fore after the Cup win, just missing out on the final, and went on to play more than 200 games for Motherwell over a decade and did a fantastic job. With Mr Reliable in your team, it was easy to sleep easy as a manager.

From a supporter's point of view, he may not have been the most exciting or eye-catching player on the park, but it would be a mistake to underestimate the role he played. I actually took him to Dundee United with me when I moved to Tannadice, which I guess is as big a compliment any manager can pay a player they have worked with in the past. I wanted Jamie in the trenches with me. He wanted to win at everything he played. It was that type of attitude, so valuable in a playing squad, that he carried into his management career in junior football. The problem was that in that line of work the lows can be as frequent as the highs and I know Jamie was a bit disillusioned after things hadn't worked out for him at Broxburn. He would phone me regularly for advice after turning to management in his own right, and I was delighted to do anything I could to help. Even as a player he was always looking to learn, he was one who would listen intently at training sessions and soak up every word of the team talk.

Had he had the opportunity over a longer period of time in coaching I've no doubt he would have found his own way, as he had that steel and determination deep inside as well as the work ethic to go with it. In many ways the circumstances of Jamie's death reflected those qualities. He was out pounding the pavements getting himself in shape for a five-a-side Masters tournament when others wouldn't have bothered to put in the effort.

Although I was out of the country, the old network came to the fore again. I spoke to Chris McCart about asking Jim Griffin to do the eulogy for Jamie, which he did. It was fitting that someone who had come through the ranks with Jamie, who had shared good times, could share his memories in that way. When we all felt it could not get any worse, the death of Paul McGrillen took us back to what was becoming a familiar place. The same emotions came flooding back.

With Davie, Phillip and Jamie there was no sense that anything could have been done to prevent their deaths. In the case of Mowgli, as Paul McGrillen was known to everyone in football, there is the nagging sense that it was avoidable. To this day I have no idea what led him to take his own life, but for anyone to reach that point it is heartbreaking. Nobody, not even those closest to Paul, had picked up on anything being amiss and he had clearly managed to mask his emotions. On the outside he was the same bubbly individual he had always been. He had the uncanny knack of being able to light up a room with his presence, the life and soul of any party. Together with Davie Cooper and Stevie Kirk he was in the thick of things in the dressing room, keeping everyone on their toes and lifting everyone's spirits.

Just as he was a lively character off the pitch, wee Mowgli had the same zest for the game as he did for life. He was an instinctive type of player. In fact, I never tired of telling him he was un-coachable.

One training session in particular sums up the man and the player. I had set out a drill working on a short throw-in routine, with the striker receiving the ball down the wing and holding off the defender to lay it back to the thrower. Mowgli took his turn as the receiver, controlling the ball before spinning past his marker and sending a shot like a rocket into the top corner of the net. As he ran past celebrating, all I picked up from the words being shouted in my general direction was, 'That wasn't bad for a throw-in.' I should have been angry, but all I could do was laugh. He was never down, always one to cheer everyone else up. That's what makes his death so difficult to comprehend. He never appeared to have a care in the world.

At the time of his death Mowgli was winding down his career with Stenhousemuir and I had been along to watch him playing at Ochilview. Still the same enthusiasm for the game, buzzing around and just loving to get shots in at goal. That was what made him tick. He could have played on longer for Motherwell but was one who was allowed to move on by Alex McLeish; in my opinion, it was too soon in Mowgli's case.

The funeral at Hamilton was devastating. I remember looking around and seeing so many familiar faces, including many of the opponents that Paul would have rubbed up the wrong way at some stage in his career. He was a real nuisance to play against, a defender's nightmare, but you didn't ever want to take that streak away from him. It was part of the compulsive type of player he was, that was the beauty of having him around. The rare ability to do something off the cuff and change a game.

He may have been a handful, but there were no enemies. People respected him for the commitment he gave to his team every time he pulled on that shirt. He was such a popular character. His wife, Michelle, was incredibly brave, as were their children, Joshua and Chloe. They did Paul proud with the way they handled the situation. To lose four players from one team in such tragic circumstances is something I don't think Scottish football has ever encountered, certainly not in my lifetime. I have to admit it has definitely affected me. With time you learn to deal with the grief, but it will always be there.

In football terms they would have been considered veterans. In the real world, they were all young men. They were dads, husbands and sons. They should still be here, still be part of family life with those nearest and dearest to them. On a personal level, I had watched each of them shed blood, sweat and tears for me in a Motherwell jersey. They put their bodies on the line to help me and their teammates achieve our goals, and I wish I had been able to tell them how much that meant to so many people. Unfortunately it is too late, with just the all too frequent reminders of those we have lost.

At Dougie Arnott's testimonial dinner there was a signed shirt from around the time of the Cup final and it was chilling to see the four signatures one beneath the other: Davie Cooper, Phillip O'Donnell, Jamie Dolan and Paul McGrillen. All written in that order.

One of the saddest realisations was that the funerals had brought us back together. Otherwise, the majority of us had gone our separate ways. Football tends to be like that, you may keep in touch with one or two people from a particular team or club but generally there is a terrible habit of losing contact. Given the experiences you share with each group, the highs and the lows that only those who have been part of it can really comprehend, everyone is guilty of not making a big enough effort on that front. What the passing of Davie, Phillip, Jamie and Paul did was put everything in perspective. Football is football, a game at the end of the day. It doesn't matter how many tens of thousands come through the gates or how much money pours in – some things are more important, and everyone involved in the sport is guilty of losing sight of that at one point or another. A visit to the Bent Cemetery in Hamilton is a reminder of that, with the graves of Coop, Phillip and Mowgli all within thirty yards of each other.

I would say I am a far more philosophical and probably a far mellower individual as a result of the horrible events over that passage of time. It set me back a bit. I think I fell out of love with football while I came to terms with everything that had happened. Time is a great healer though, and I came to realise that football was not to blame. It was simply the common thread that had brought us all together. For that, I'm grateful.

16

THE ROAD TO HAMPDEN

Who are you hoping for when the draw is made? If I had a pound for every time I had been asked that question as a football manager I'd be a wealthy man. It is the stock question at every stage of every Cup competition up and down the land. The diplomatic answer is to say there are no easy ties but a home draw would be preferable. Deep down, what every coach is hoping for is, sure enough, a game at their own ground, but what they'll never admit to is that there are definitely teams they would rather play. Teams they know that nine times out of ten they will get a win against.

When the draw for the Scottish Cup third round was made in the 1990/91 season I was like every other Premier Division manager entering the competition at that stage and hoping for a nice, gentle introduction. Celtic, to pick just one, were handed what on paper looked like a palatable enough tie-up at Forfar. Dundee United were making the short trip to East Fife as red-hot favourites. Me? I was preparing to face the Scottish Cup holders, Aberdeen, in front of more than 10,000 Dons fans at Pittodrie. As far as teams I would have preferred to have avoided go, I would say they would have been pretty much at the top of the list.

So it was with a degree of trepidation that we boarded the bus and made our way north. Under Alex Smith they were a well-organised team with a very decent bank of creativity in all of the key areas, so what we couldn't afford to do was try to sit in and aim for a replay at Fir Park. We had to fight fire with fire, and we did that for large chunks of the game. Chance after chance went begging and you start to think it isn't going to be your day – and then you send for Stevie Kirk. He wouldn't thank anyone for being labelled a Super Sub, and in truth he was much more than that. Stevie started more games than he played in from the bench, but because of the impact he so often made as a replacement there has been that perception of him.

In the Aberdeen game, at least, I think the Super Sub tag can justifiably be applied. There cannot have been many more dramatic introductions to a game than when Stevie appeared in the second half to face the Dons. We made the switch after play had broken for a free kick to us midway inside the Dons half. Davie Cooper was over the ball and had to hold his fire until we could get Stevie on to the park. As he ran on, he made a beeline for Davie and had a quick word before jogging on to take up his position in the middle of the park. Then Coop could get on with the job in the hand, but as he shaped to shoot he instead rolled a short ball square across the park for Stevie to step forward and rifle an incredible shot past Theo Snelders in the Aberdeen goal. Snelders got a hand to the ball, but there was no way he was going to keep it out. It was the one and only goal of the game but it was certainly worthy of winning any match – not a bad first touch!

It was no more than we deserved, having been unlucky on a number of occasions that afternoon, with Davie pulling the strings and rolling back the years. It took a moment of magic from Stevie to break down the barriers and at the other end we were able to keep out the highly fancied Dons team. Maybe at that point we should have started to think it was going to be our year, but the focus is always on the next tie, you just don't dare to look beyond that. In our case, Falkirk at Fir Park was what came out of the hat.

After Aberdeen it should have been a welcome one for us, but the fact they were flying high in the First Division and on course for the championship ensured there was absolutely no prospect of us taking our eye off the ball. As anticipated, it was far from a straightforward tie. Nick Cusack gave us an early lead, but Sammy McGivern levelled it. It was still close going into the second half but after the break wee Joe McLeod scored to put us back in front. That should have been that, but Falkirk hit back with a really well worked second goal by Alex Taylor and it was back to square one. Then it was time for Stevie Kirk to step forward with his customary goal, which he duly did. Another from Cusack towards the end took us over the finish line and what could have been a real banana skin of a tie had been safely negotiated.

The fifth round paired me with my old side, Morton, and again I was prepared for a battle, born out by the fact we drew 0–0 in the first game at Fir Park and then 1–1 in the return at Cappielow. We eventually went through on penalties, but it hadn't half been a struggle. That game in Greenock was notable for a couple of reasons, one everyone who was there on the night will remember and the other that very few will be aware of. Firstly, it was the match in which John Gahagan threatened to break Motherwell hearts. I'd let John go at the time I'd brought Joe McLeod in from Dundee United, and after ten years at the club he was a popular character. If anyone was going to score against us that night I suppose I should have guessed it would be him, and sure enough, he did, equalising after we'd taken the lead and generally putting in the type of performance that must have left our fans wondering why he wasn't still with us.

John's better known now for his work on the comedy and after-dinner speaking circuit, something I wouldn't have predicted in a million years. He was quiet as a mouse during his playing days; he rarely spoke. To see him go on to make his living from being up on stage was incredible, but I was delighted for John. Anyone who has seen him in action as a speaker will tell you he's made for the job. He had worked on in football as a community coach in the Central Belt when he eventually made the leap and went full-time on the entertainment scene.

John's role in the Cup tie was one significant part of the Morton tie, but so too was the guest list for the evening. Included on the list for complimentary tickets were representatives from Nottingham Forest and Chelsea, and I had no doubt it was Motherwell they had come to watch. We had a number of good young players and the scouts were beginning to circle, paying particular attention to Tommy Boyd. It transpired that it was indeed Boyd who was centre of attention, and he didn't do his chances of a move any harm with his performance on what was a dirty-looking night, with horrible conditions. Tam was revelling in the opportunity to play alongside Davie Cooper and the two of them struck up a great understanding. It was that relationship that put us ahead, with the pair linking up well in the build-up and then Tam carrying on his run to get on the end of a typical Coop cross to head home the opening goal of the game.

He had a good game, aside from losing Gahagan for their goal, and straight after the match I had word that both Forest and Chelsea were keen to meet. I went through to Glasgow and held talks with both clubs, hoping that I would at least be able to keep hold of him until the end of the season. Agents were beginning to make their presence felt and when you had competition between two sides it was another complication.

Brian Clough was there for Forest and Bobby Campbell was

there with his Chelsea hat on, very different characters, but both had the ability to be persuasive and they weren't keen on leaving without getting their man. From a selfish point of view, I was hoping the Forest move didn't come off. They were still going strong in the FA Cup and as long as they had a chance of winning silverware they were keen to get Tam in straight away. It turned out to be the year they went on to reach the final, losing to Tottenham. Chelsea, on the other hand, were quite content to leave Tam to play out the season with us and then take him in the summer if he agreed to move to Stamford Bridge.

Brian was a straight talker and a pleasure to deal with. He was a football man through and through and you couldn't doubt his passion. I was also left in no doubt about how desperate he was to get Tam to the City Ground. Chelsea too were very enthusiastic and in the end it was London, not Nottingham, that Tam plumped for after talking at length to both clubs. It brought back memories for me, having been in a similar position as a young player with Kilmarnock.

I hadn't felt London was right for me, but Tam was attracted to the prospect of a move south and got good vibes from Chelsea. He went on to spend just a season at Stamford Bridge and I was surprised he didn't get more time to make an impact – although it worked out for him in the end, as he got his move back to Scotland with Celtic and never looked back. Tam leaned towards Celtic and when I realised he was looking to come home, I thought it was perfect for him. He always caught the eye going forward and with the Old Firm teams you tend to get that opportunity, even as a defender. I got a real fillip from watching the way he grew and developed from the young boy who we had first seen at Motherwell. He had started as a sweeper as a kid and I also played him in midfield before settling on him as a full-back, where I thought he was better suited to playing, as he was more comfortable moving onto the ball than being in front of the play.

He also deserved the rewards that came with his big moves, considering the pittance he was paid at Motherwell. That was why we never stood in anyone's way, because there was no way we could compete with the salaries on offer elsewhere. We agreed a fee of £800,000 with Chelsea and also brokered a deal for the transfer to be delayed until the summer. It gave us a final few months with Tam in the side, particularly important given the progress we were making in the Scottish Cup at that period and something we had always been keen to ensure.

Tam was a gem to work with and I have a lot of respect for what he achieved in the game and the way he conducted himself throughout his career. He's proof positive that if you work hard and apply yourself properly then the opportunities will follow. Chelsea may not have turned out to be the dream move that he had hoped for, but it did pave the way for his switch to Celtic and nobody would argue against the plaudits that went Tam's way in later years. I always followed his progress with a keen eye and to see him going from strength to strength in Scotland colours was fantastic for everyone at Motherwell. We put our hearts and souls into looking after young players the right way and giving them a good grounding in the professional game.

The decision to choose Chelsea ahead of Forest ensured Tam would be with us for the remaining games of the Cup campaign, a major boost for us at a time when the squad was tight. We ran with the bare minimum of senior players and losing one as influential as him would have been a blow.

Motherwell went in to the pot for the semi-final draw alongside Celtic, Dundee United and St Johnstone. Who was I hoping for when the draw was made? In truth, anyone but Celtic. They were off the pace in terms of the championship, with Rangers and Aberdeen leading the pack, but playing either of the Old Firm in a semi-final is never going to be a walk in the park. Needless to say, the draw put us up against Celtic. It was one of those years when everything, on paper at least, appeared to go against us. We certainly weren't getting an easy ride.

We went in to the semi-final without Davie Cooper, who was injured, and that certainly dented our chances of imposing ourselves on a Celtic team that didn't lack in quality of its own. John Collins was a thorn in our side, although we handled him well enough on the day. It was a nervy afternoon. We survived a few scares, not least when Chris McCart had to look sharp to clear a shot off the line but on the other hand had a decent shout for a penalty when Dougie Arnott was brought down in the box. The claims were waved away and I remember thinking at that moment that our chance had gone – you don't tend to get too many opportunities against the big two.

We held on to the end, working hard to match them all the way, but after the doing we had received in the first half of that match we had to think ourselves lucky. In all honesty, we could have been three or four down, but we got the breaks you need and hung on in there. John Chapman, the chairman, was quite delighted with the prospect of a replay. The four teams in the semi-finals shared the gate money equally from those two games, but the money from the second match against Celtic was to be split between the two of us. From a financial perspective it was the perfect outcome, but it wasn't the best for my nerves! If we could have had it done and dusted inside ninety minutes it would have been ideal, but to be still in the Cup was the main thing. I always felt we had a chance, even as underdogs in the eyes of everyone watching from the outside. It was a gutsy group of players, not to mention a talented bunch, and we certainly didn't fear any team.

In the initial tie against Celtic we hadn't done ourselves justice, so the incentive was there to go out and prove what we were made of. We might have expected the replay to be a similarly cagey affair – it turned out to be anything but, with six goals and no shortage of drama. It was a tremendous advert for Cup football and the supporters got their money's worth when they bought their tickets for that particular game, there's no question about that.

By the time we went into that game we knew that Dundee United had made it past St Johnstone to book their place in the final. That didn't particularly impact on our approach to the game or performance on the night, but I would be lying if at the back of my mind I didn't appreciate how significant it would be for my brother and I to be facing each other at Hampden. Mind you, I didn't have much time to give that any thought when the game was up and running – there were goals flying in left, right and centre. Paul Elliot had given Celtic the lead early on, but Dougie Arnott brought us back into the game when he reacted the quickest inside the box after an Ian Angus shot had broken to him. Dougie terrorised big defenders and was an important part of what we achieved that season, not just for his semi-final contribution.

Unfortunately the parity didn't last for long. Anton Rogan, not exactly the most frequent of goal scorers, was the man who did the damage and put us in at half-time 2–1 down. We had forty-five minutes to turn things around and the break provided us a chance to regroup and focus on what needed to be done. We'd given Celtic too much respect in the first period, we had to start playing our own game and making the most of what we had in our locker. In short, those players in a claret and amber shirt had to believe they were the ones who deserved to be running out at Hampden in the final. That is what I'd asked them to do and to a man they answered me in some style. Dougie Arnott, with a wonderful header, made it 2–2.

Then *that* goal was scored. Colin O'Neill hit an absolute rasper into the top corner from way out, one of the goals of the season in anyone's book. It was fairy-tale stuff for Colin, one to replay for the grandkids in years to come and a strike that any football supporter of a certain age will remember as vividly as though it happened yesterday. At 3–2 you're always vulnerable and obviously defences hadn't exactly been on top, so when Stevie Kirk did the needful and made it 4–2 at last there was a chance to take a breath and start to think that it might just be our night. It was a lovely curling shot, another one to savour in a game that no Motherwell supporter will ever forget.

As a player I had taken part in more semi-finals than I can remember and been fortunate to have had more than my share of Cup final experiences. As a manager it was a very different set of emotions when the whistle sounded and we knew we were going to Hampden – relief and joy, but, more than anything, a huge sense of pride.

Motherwell had been the nearly men on so many occasions and I know the supporters were beginning to feel their day in the sunshine might never come. The Cup final was for them and for a special group of players and it was a privilege to have played a part in making that happen.

17

HEROES ARE BORN

Amid all the heartache and worry behind the scenes for Jim and I, following the death of our father and the scare regarding Beth's pregnancy, we never lost sight of the fact there was a game of football to be played and a trophy to be won. That was what we were paid to do by our clubs and that was what we both set out to do on 18 May 1991. Sometimes in a Cup final the pressure can get to you and the result is a pain in the tonsil type of game. This one was different, though. The crowd had made for a different type of atmosphere and there wasn't the same tension that there so often is.

Jim had lost five Scottish Cup finals and there were some survivors from those games in his team for 1991, with Maurice Malpas, Dave Bowman and Jim McInally among them. They were experienced campaigners and were hurting from their Cup final experiences previously, so we knew how dangerous United would be. For me, it was my first as a manager and brought a new kind of burden for me. Picking a team becomes second nature, but in Cup final week it is far removed from the norm.

There was one main dilemma when it came to selecting the side to face United – Craig Paterson or John Philliben in the centre of the defence. John had done really well during the Cup run, but I was wary of Darren Jackson's pace. Craig was the faster of the two options, so I went with him. It was a hammer blow for John, not an easy one to take, but to his credit he was very professional about it. I still feel for him now, but I did what I felt was best for the team. As a manager those are the most difficult decisions to make, the ones that are borderline and that will impact on a player's life.

The other big decision to make was whether to go for Stevie Kirk or Iain Ferguson from the start. My thought on that one was that we had to try and pin Maurice Malpas back as much as possible and prevent him from making the type of run forward that would have damaged us, so Iain was better suited to that type of work in the first instance. Iain's instinct was to go forward, so it meant Malpas would have been concentrating on his defensive duties. Stevie, as I've said before, was always a very valuable player coming off the bench and the Cup final was made for that. They both had a role to play at different stages in the match.

By the eve of the match your preparation is done. The main task is to keep the focus and make sure everyone is in the right frame of mind. We had gone through a session on Thursday at Fir Park, then the main one on the Friday in Ayr to run through the final shaping. I always prepared Team A and Team B, in the main something designed to keep the players guessing. You didn't want to make it too easy for those who were going to be starting, to guard against complacency, and at the same time didn't want to leave those who wouldn't be playing feeling too low.

I named the team on Saturday morning, as I normally would have done, giving me time to explain what was required of those who were playing. We had our lunch at the hotel in Irvine before boarding the coach for the trip north. We travelled up just after noon on the Saturday, with that journey as important as any other part of the build-up as far as I was concerned. With that in mind, I hadn't left anything to chance and managed to get hold of a soundtrack I hoped would give us an edge. It wasn't an inspirational compilation or some sort of high-energy music. Instead it was a classical mix, not your usual dressing room choice. It had come from Ross Mathie, who was coaching as part of the SFA's youth set-up at that point, and was doing the rounds across the world. Was Scotland ready for it? I thought it was at least worth a try. The idea was to give the players some peaceful music to contemplate what lay ahead for them, the calm before the storm. It wasn't quite whale music, but probably just one stop away from it.

I told them, 'Take five minutes to relax.' I'm pretty sure the vast majority of the guys on that coach, if not all of them, thought I'd finally lost my marbles. I could see the likes of Colin O'Neill, Stevie Kirk and Davie Cooper staring at me and just waiting for the chance to rip me to shreds. I'm not for a second saying the tape was a huge part of what we did that day, but I'll stick to my guns and say I definitely think it was worth a try. Anything that might give you an edge can't be ignored. It gave the players a chance to reflect and calmed things right down at a time when the excitement was reaching fever pitch.

It is a long, long day and anything to break that up is a good thing. We'd done the team talk back at the hotel, had breakfast and gone for a walk around the grounds to pass a bit of time. The good thing is it was just a forty-five-minute drive up the road to Hampden, so the wait was almost over. The last five minutes of that journey were the most inspiring – even for me, having played at the Bernabeu and Nou Camp, it sent a tingle down my spine to see the crowds beginning to form and the stadium looming large. It is just a unique day to be involved in.

The team lines were all written up and handed in when we

arrived, but the biggest distraction was dealing with the complimentary tickets. Having been away for a few days, a lot of the players were still handling requests on the day of the match and had to dish them out. It was amazing how time consuming that all became, with people sorting out payments and all the rest.

The allocation was split down the middle and seats were snapped up. Motherwell had never had a crowd like that. It was amazing. People like to be associated with success and once you get to Hampden everyone comes out, from the youngest kids through to the grannies and granddads. It was just an incredible occasion for everyone with a connection to Motherwell.

The challenge for us was to try and keep things as near to normal as we possibly could. Working with me for the final I had Tam Forsyth, Cammy Murray, masseur Tom Pringle, and Bobby Holmes, who was the trainer and physio. They were a great team to work with, each with a part to play. While they did their thing, I took the chance to take a walk out on the park and gather my thoughts. It would be great to be able to say that I had a momentous team talk planned and that was what won us the Cup. The truth of the matter is that it was completely off the cuff, nothing elaborate or at all scientific. The important work had been done in the week leading up to the game and that morning when we had gathered together at the hotel to run through the team and final plans.

Before kick-off it was a case of keeping things simple, direct and reinforcing what we had spoken about already. At that stage you don't want to be crowding the minds of the players, although I did like to take time out to speak to each individually to let them know exactly what was expected of them. It was only a couple of minutes with each player, but a very important couple of minutes. The main ones I needed to get through to were the old heads, those who I'd be relying on most. Davie Cooper and Craig Paterson fell into that category, two I needed to be my eyes and ears on the pitch and to help drive the youngsters on if the going got tough. You need to have leaders of men on the pitch and in Davie and Craig I had that – they had been over the course umpteen times before. Tam Boyd was another who fitted the bill. Even as a younger player he was a big influence.

Going in to the Cup final, we were losing the season's games against Dundee United 3–1 in terms of wins. We had a lot of ground to make up. As I mentioned, the pace of Darren Jackson was my greatest concern but we also had the very different threat of Duncan Ferguson to contend with. He was still young and erratic, but at the same time he had the height and power to trouble any defender. With Jackson, the intention was to use Craig Paterson's pace to cancel him out. For dealing with Duncan Ferguson, the instruction was very much to cut the crosses out at source and prevent the balls from coming into the box.

Whilst we were aware of that twin-pronged attack, the early part of the match saw the danger coming from two of the other United players. Hamish French actually had the ball in the back of the net but the referee Davie Syme chalked it off – it was a very close offside decision, but you don't complain when those go in your favour. Then Freddy van der Hoorn stepped forward and fired in a shot that rattled off the post and flew across the face of goal. Again it was a case of breathing a sigh of relief, and I remember thinking it could be a case of déjà-vu, with echoes of the game against Celtic in the semi-final when we survived a few scares to go on and win.

In those early stages there's no doubt United were pressing harder than we were. On our side there was a more cautious, possibly nervous, start. But we began to feel our way in and start to cause problems of our own. Before long it looked as though both sets of players had forgotten the pressure of the day and thrown the shackles off. It turned into a really open and entertaining affair.

Chris McCart and Craig Paterson were both unlucky not to put us ahead and, eventually, with thirty minutes on the clock, we made the breakthrough. It was a fantastic goal, certainly worthy of the occasion, with Iain Ferguson playing in Jim Griffin down the right and his deep cross picking out Fergie's run into the box and hanging perfectly for a lovely header to fly into the back of the net.

We settled things down after that, concentrating on playing our own game, and took it through to half-time. My message was to keep it simple, keep the concentration and to push for opportunities to give ourselves a bit more of a cushion. Then it all changed with a clattering bang just ten minutes after the break. When John Clark crashed through Ally Maxwell, it looked in an instant as though all of our good work would be undone. John was a big beast of a man and it was no contest between him and Ally, who crumpled to the ground. I thought it was a bad challenge, but Ally was basically given no protection by the referee. He was left with broken ribs and what would later be found to be a ruptured spleen. It was heavy-duty stuff. At the time we knew it was a serious injury but had no idea of the gravity of it or the potential consequences. Instead, the focus was on patching Ally up and keeping him on the park.

The Cup rules only allowed for two substitutes, so I didn't have a keeper on the bench. I was tempted to put Stevie Kirk in as he'd done it before, but I didn't want to show my hand too early. Ally said he could soldier on and we went with that. It was a long, long second half. Bobby Holmes stood behind the goal and at every opportunity was working on Ally, trying his best to keep him going. All I could really do was keep an eye on the situation and keep my fingers crossed that he would be able to see it through.

Perhaps not surprisingly, we conceded an equaliser not long after. A long and low shot from Davie Bowman from outside the box fizzed past Ally, who was always going to find it difficult to get down to anything along the turf given the pain he was in. The key was to try and regroup, retain possession and work harder than ever to keep the ball away from our own box. United knew our weakness and if they had any opportunity I've no doubt John Clark and Duncan Ferguson would have been looking to go in hard and test Ally again.

The best form of defence is attack and we were keen to peg United back in their own half. We did that in style, scoring twice in the process. The first came from a typically accurate Davie Cooper free kick, floated in to the back post for it to be nodded back across goal to tee up Phillip O'Donnell's brave header. Young Phillip threw himself at the ball, through a ruck of bodies, and got his reward. Ian Angus put us 3–1 ahead with a tremendous shot from outside the box, coming from a Stevie Kirk lay-off. Stevie had just been thrown on from the bench and, as usual, didn't take long to make an impact.

With a two-goal lead we were looking good value to go on and win the Cup, but I knew better than anyone that Jim and his team wouldn't give up on it until the last ball had been kicked. Sure enough, United came back at us and it was one of their substitutes that dragged them back into the game – John O'Neil scoring with a good header to bring it back to 3–2. The drama wasn't finished and a huge Alan Main clearance caused all sorts of problems, with Darren Jackson nipping in to get the run on Craig Paterson and in ahead of Ally Maxwell to head home the equaliser. It wasn't lost on me that I'd taken Craig in to cope with

Darren's pace and he was left standing for that one, the best laid plans don't always work out.

The prospect of extra-time with a goalkeeper who was clearly toiling didn't fill me with joy, but we still had a chance of lifting that cup. That was the main thing at that stage.

For the first time, the prospect of penalties was looming large in my mind. Would it have been fair to expect Ally to face a shoot-out? I wasn't convinced and was tempted to switch things around in extra-time to put Stevie Kirk in for the closing stages and penalties. He had gone in as a stopgap against Hearts previously and saved a spot kick, so he had form.

I never lost faith that we would get there in the end and it was maybe written in the stars that it would be Kirky, a talisman right the way through that run, who would get the decisive goal. When a Davie Cooper corner from the right wound its way through to Stevie at the back post he was calm enough to head it home with real composure. If he was cool, the supporters in the stands were anything but – the celebrations were straight from the heart, pure joy.

It wasn't cut and dried, right down to the closing seconds. Ally had to perform heroics to turn away a Maurice Malpas shot – had he been fully fit it would have been an exceptional save, but given the extent of the damage he had suffered it was nothing short of miraculous.

It was only after the match that we found out how serious it was, with Ally whisked away to hospital and the tests revealing the damage to his spleen. It could have had unthinkable consequences and there is no way in the world he should have played on in those circumstances, but the adrenalin obviously kicked in. You have to be led by your players and when Ally said he was able to carry on we took him at his word. If there had been any indication that he had ruptured his spleen he would have been hooked off the park straight away and put in the back of an ambulance. He showed a lot of heart that afternoon and throughout that team there were players who fought like lions to take the cup back to Fir Park. There were no disappointments on the day, just phenomenal displays in every area of the pitch. They deserve their place as Motherwell legends.

18

LAYING THE FOUNDATIONS

When you look at the managerial churn in football today, it would be easy to be fooled into thinking success should be expected overnight. In practical terms, particularly when money is tight, that simply isn't the case. Our Scottish Cup win in '91 is the perfect illustration of the patience required to build a team and a squad capable of competing for honours, with the first blocks put in place seven years before Motherwell's name was engraved on the trophy.

The making of the side went right back to the start of the 1980s, when the longest-serving members of that team came together as youngsters. Ally Maxwell was one of those who had come through the Fir Park Boys Club set-up and had been a part-time player at one stage. I'd actually taken in John Gardiner from Dundee United with a view to being my No.1, but in time Ally pushed his way to the front of the queue with his impressive performances as he came through the ranks. Luc Nijholt was the other side of the coin, an import new addition to the Scottish game. Luc was one of those we brought in from the continent, although it was under freedom of contract rather than with a weighty fee attached. It was the first time we had used the agent Ton van Dalen, who was making a name for himself as a very good operator. He certainly didn't disappoint with Luc, who was a very strong defender and a good user of the ball.

The Dutch market was one that was accessible for clubs like Motherwell, but the caveat was that I always liked to see the players on Scottish soil before committing. You need to see them in the environment in which they will be working, whether they fit in with the squad and the way of life. The only issue we had was the expectation that the club would pick up the bill for everything, including housing. I found myself looking around Hamilton and Bothwell to get accommodation for them, so turned my hand to becoming an estate agent as well as a football manager. Jim's solution at Dundee United was to buy a house and employ a landlady to look after the overseas players, but we stopped short of that.

By taking care of those details and doing the right homework before committing to a signing, the hope was that the risk was taken out of signing players from overseas. It didn't always work that way and some, for example Bart Verhuel, didn't settle. Bart came in from Holland but was young and coming away from home for the first time. He didn't fulfil the potential he had and ended up going back home after just a handful of first-team games. You win some, you lose some. Luc was certainly a winner for us and picked up a Cup medal for his troubles.

Chris McCart was another of the youth products. He was in with the bricks at Fir Park and a very loyal servant over the years. I watched him grow and mature into a top-class player, one who was a role model for those who followed in later years.

Craig Paterson was at the other end of the age range and was one I had taken in from Rangers. I was there when John Greig had signed him from Hibs and he enjoyed success at Ibrox, albeit during difficult years. Injuries prevented Craig from getting a good clean run of games on a regular basis and by the time

Graeme Souness came in it was the end of the road for him there. Regardless of any concerns about his fitness, Craig was a good reader of the game and a good talker out on the pitch. He's put that talent to good use on the radio since hanging up his boots.

If Craig was nearing the end of his time at the top level, Tam Boyd was just a youngster in comparison. He was another who had been reared through our youth system and it was with a real sense of pride that they went out and made their own way in the world. Jim Griffin, playing on the right side of the midfield, was another one of the Motherwell Boys' Club graduates and well versed in what the club was all about. He was on great form in the Cup final, typical of the job he did on such a regular basis. Ian Angus was a rarity, a player we had gone out and bought. Ian had been at Aberdeen, where he was a Premier Division winner, and then went on to have a spell at Dundee before I managed to tempt him south. He did a real turn for me. Phillip O'Donnell was another local lad who had come good and worked his socks off to get his chance. Once he got that, Phillip carried on working and looking towards the next goal. He hated standing still.

Davie Cooper, as mentioned previously, was the best £50,000 I ever spent. That piece of business, getting a legend to commit to our future, was the turning point for the club. Dougie Arnott came in from Pollok Juniors for all of £1,500 and made the transition quite quickly, adapting to the pace of the senior game but also revelling in the fact he had quality players around him. Iain Ferguson completed the eleven on the day, and he was another one who we had dipped into our pockets for. It cost us in the region of £75,000 to bring Iain across from Hearts, and once we did that it gave us an extra element to our play, a little more goal threat and a direct physical presence.

On the bench we had Stevie Kirk and Colin O'Neill, two guys

from different backgrounds but both heroes to the Motherwell supporters. Stevie was signed from East Fife for £27,000 and proved to be a bargain. His contribution in the Cup run alone made him worth ten times that amount, but it was his value off the pitch too that made him such a great signing. He lifted the spirits and was a joy to have around the club. Colin came to us as a youngster from Northern Ireland, where he had been playing with Portadown. We paid £15,000, and the first thing we had to do was get him fit and help him shed a few pounds, but he was always a big physical presence. He didn't get the nickname Psycho for no reason ... he relished getting involved in the midfield battles.

Including Colin in the Cup final squad was a bit of gamble, as he'd been struggling with a knee injury, but he gave me a good option for shoring things up if need be so I went with my instinct. He'd actually been well on the road to recovery but had been set back a bit when he got a bang on the knee in the swimming pool at the hotel before the final, which obviously wasn't ideal. Colin was another of the characters in the dressing room. He got into his fair share of scrapes on the park but you forgave him that because of what he brought to the team.

All in all, it wasn't an expensive team to put together, but it proved to be very effective. Versatility was one of the key qualities, with quite a few players capable of playing more than one position and playing it well. Luc Nijholt was comfortable across the defence or in midfield, Ian Angus was happy on either wing or at full-back, while Jim Griffin was at home anywhere down the right-hand side. That gave me a lot of scope, even when working with a small squad.

For all of the quality I had in that group, what I knew was that, as soon as the cup had been brought to Fir Park, I had to start rebuilding what was a winning side. Some of it was enforced change. Some of it was by choice. I wasn't prepared to rest on our laurels and knew the areas I needed to refresh to make sure we kept progressing. No matter how attached you are to a group of players, it isn't sensible to let things go stale. You have to keep evolving. It became part of my routine on a Monday to have a look for teams that had suffered a poor result and see if there were players in that side that I was interested in. If there was someone in there, it was the perfect time to strike, as more often than not you'd find a manager who was still sore from the result on the Saturday and only too happy to move players on. It worked many times for me over the years.

At the same time, the matter of players moving in the opposite direction was another facet of the day job. Tam Boyd was the first of the Cup-winning team to move on, with his move to Chelsea already agreed before the Cup final. After that there was a steady enough stream of comings and goings. Looking through the Cup final team, it's interesting to see how such a close-knit team began to break up.

Ally Maxwell remained for less than a year after his courageous efforts in the Cup final. I know an agent had been advising Ally and I think he'd had his head turned, and we ended up sending him out on loan, firstly to Liverpool and then Bolton. Eventually he got his move to Rangers. While I was disappointed at the time, in hindsight I can appreciate it was Ally's chance to get a big move at a stage in his career that probably meant it would be his last major transfer.

Luc Nijholt stayed for a couple of seasons after the Cup final before he was bought by Swindon for £175,000, which for us was good business. With the overseas players I never bargained for having them around for more than a season or two, as the natural trend was for them to look towards getting back to their home country by then.

Chris McCart remained at Fir Park long beyond me, eventually moving on to Falkirk in 1997, but Craig Paterson followed Tam Boyd out of the door in the aftermath of the Cup final. Craig was out of contract and we couldn't agree terms for him to stay, so he shifted to Kilmarnock – although I was the last to know about that. In the end we needed a tribunal to set the fee, which came in at £50,000. For a player of his experience, on the back of a Cup win, it was weighted in Killie's favour.

Ian Angus stayed for another three years, moving on to Clyde after I had left the club, and Jim Griffin played on for the remainder of my time at Fir Park too. A knee injury forced Jim to call it a day, but he stayed on the coaching staff under Alex McLeish. Phillip O'Donnell had an integral part to play in the three years between the Cup success and his dream move to Celtic, with Davie Cooper's stay at Motherwell also lasting until 1994.

Iain Ferguson was another who was still tied to the club, moving on to Airdrie two years after his Hampden exploits, while Dougie Arnott never left. It wasn't until injury led to his retirement in 1998 that Dougie finally dropped out of the Motherwell team after being a fixture for well over a decade.

Stevie Kirk was among those moved on after I left the manager's job, but Colin O'Neill was another who had to call it a day early due to injury. He battled away for a year after we won the trophy trying to get himself fit and ready, but had to concede defeat eventually.

That, in a nutshell, is how the making and breaking of the Cup-winning team ran its course. It was never my intention for the journey to stop at Hampden. We had to keep moving forward and aiming high. Within a few years, the dream of going one better than winning the Cup very nearly became reality.

19

BUILDING FOR THE FUTURE

The euphoria in Motherwell in 1991 was something to behold. Even with the turmoil in my home life, I was able to take a step back and soak in what it meant to the people of the town. The Cup win was such a huge high, but away from football there was the terrible low of the situation at Ravenscraig. With the works being wound down to closure, nearly 800 hardworking men and women were set to lose their jobs – not to mention the thousands who were employed by companies supporting the steel plant. It was a devastating blow for Lanarkshire and when Ravenscraig finally closed a year after the Cup final, it was the end of a way of life for so many people.

Just as my father's death had put the Cup final into perspective for me personally, I tried to use the situation at the steel works to put it into perspective for the players. Despite the fact people were worried for their future, for the jobs that put food on the table, they were still putting their hands in their pockets and paying through the gate to watch Motherwell play. We had 10,000 at Fir Park for the quarter-final tie against Morton, which would have been a tremendous crowd under any circumstances, but given the economic situation in the area it was phenomenal.

I told the squad they had a responsibility to those supporters to make sure the money they spent to back the team wasn't wasted. We owed it to them to repay them and the best way to do that was by winning games. There's no way to compensate someone for having their life torn apart by redundancy, but I hope in a small way the Cup win at least gave a bit of joy to brighten a dark time for the town. It was a significant win on so many levels, not least financially for Motherwell Football Club. Prior to the final against Dundee United we were still very much in debt, but the combination of our share of the gate receipts, the prize money, sponsorship and everything associated with winning the Cup, as well as the proceeds of Tam Boyd's move to Chelsea, pushed us back into the black for the first time since I had joined seven years earlier.

When I had arrived in 1984 the level of debt was potentially crippling. It was very much a fight for survival. By being sensible in our approach to spending and by pulling in transfer fee after transfer fee we had turned that around and were able to make ground improvements along the way, creating Fir Park as we know it now. That was as satisfying as winning the trophy itself.

I was heavily involved in the financial model, joining the board in 1987 to ensure I had a voice at that level. We worked to a comprehensive set of projections and carried out monthly audits to make sure we weren't slipping back into the ways of old. Back then the likes of Peter Marinello had been signed, players who were out of the wage bracket that a club the size of Motherwell could afford. That was what put the club in the grubber and our job was to pull it back out. Realism was the cornerstone of the business plan. We had somewhere in the region of 35,000 supporters turning out for the Cup final, but the first game of the following season brought in just 4,500 at Fir Park, so that was ultimately the core we had to rely upon in terms of ongoing gate receipts.

I found it bizarre and sad to watch from the outside as John Boyle came in and started signing players that the crowd figures didn't reflect, the John Spencers and Andy Gorams of this world on big money. That undid all the good work we had done and led Motherwell into administration, something that was unthinkable when we had money in the bank and a cup in the trophy cabinet. Billy Davies, who had seen it from both sides as a player during the more prudent times and as manager in later years, always said I would have fainted if I'd seen the wage bill from his time in charge. The chairman, John Chapman, was brilliant at ensuring we lived within our means and it was a real shame that wasn't maintained.

The financial stability we established in the wake of the Cup win allowed me to move into an area of the transfer market that had been out of bounds up to that point. It was far from a war chest, but there was at least scope to bolster the squad with players of a very good standard. To put it in context, Aberdeen were signing players of the calibre of Charlie Nicholas and Hans Gilhaus – international strikers with big reputations – so we were by no means operating on a level playing field financially. Instead we had to try and be sharper and cleverer, looking for gems in the rough. Brian Martin was one of those we invested in, spending £180,000 to bring him to Fir Park from St Mirren. Brian could play right-back, left-back or at centre-half – an out-and-out defender who loved that part of the game, but who was capable of taking the ball forward. He went on to justify our faith in him, earning a place in the Scotland squad in time.

Rab McKinnon was another of the new recruits who went on to play for the national side, just as well after I put my neck on the line to sign him . . . going down on Boxing Day to watch him play for Hartlepool, taking pelters from Beth, as you might expect, for working over Christmas. I drove down to see them playing Bradford and bumped into Joe Jordan, who was in charge at Hearts at that point, at the ground. I knew Joe was watching Rab too, so pretty early into the match I told him there was nothing for me in either team and made my exit. In truth I'd seen enough to make my mind up that I wanted Rab, but I didn't want to push Joe into making his move early, to try and buy myself a bit of time.

I knew Rab had been on trial at Manchester United, so took the opportunity to talk to Archie Knox and Alex Ferguson about him. They were impressed with his ability but had concerns about his build, feeling he was a bit heavy and not mobile enough to play for United at the highest level. I always liked to get background information on everyone I signed, and a reference from Old Trafford wasn't a bad starting point. If they were impressed, it was good enough for me.

Paul Lambert was another future Scotland star we identified and brought to Motherwell. Paul cost £100,000 from St Mirren and was as good a recruit as I expected he would be. He had won the Scottish Cup as a youngster with St Mirren under Alex Smith and when I spoke to Alex at the time we signed him, he was very positive. What he did recommend was that when I went to watch him in action, to avoid reserve games. Alex's opinion was that Paul always faired better when he was in the first team, with better players around him. In reserve games he didn't tend to shine, as he wasn't a flamboyant type of player. That was something that was borne out when he moved to the continent and slotted in perfectly comfortably in a very talented Borussia Dortmund team – able to raise his own game to excel.

Winning the Champions League wasn't at the forefront of Paul's mind when he agreed to join Motherwell, but he always had the ability to go on to great things. I liked a midfield with three components: a player to win the ball, one to pass the ball and one to support the front men. In Jamie Dolan, Paul Lambert and Phillip O'Donnell I had those three, in that order.

Of course, not every signing was a success, and in some cases you simply can't second guess how things will work out. Colin McNair is the perfect example of a player who didn't make the most of the ability he had. Colin had actually come through the youth ranks at Falkirk, but I took him across to Motherwell in November 1989 as a promising centre-half or midfield player who I thought I could help improve. I never really had a chance with Colin, though. There were other things in his life that seemed more important to him than his career in football, and when that's the case you just can't really compete.

What summed it all up for me was when we came back to Fir Park from training one day and discovered all four of the tyres on his car had been slashed while it was left parked at the ground. Naturally my first reaction was to get the police involved, but Colin was insistent he didn't want that. Straight away the alarm bells were ringing and it didn't take a genius to put two and two together. He was a Glasgow boy and was involved with a bad crowd, even at that young age. Why they'd come looking for him I don't know for sure, but the knife in the tyres was obviously a warning to him about something. The suspicion at the time was that it was the drug gangs from the city that had come out looking for Colin, but we couldn't prove that and he certainly didn't want to talk to anyone at the club about it.

That was just one of the scrapes he got into while he was on our books, with the final straw coming in training when he got involved in a scuffle with Paul McGrillen during training. Jim Griffin jumped in to separate the two but ended up coming off worst and I had no option but to show Colin the door. He ended up at Albion Rovers afterwards but was already in a downward spiral, charged with possessing heroin with intent to supply in 1992. At later court appearances it was said he was so addicted to heroin that he had taken to stealing from his own family, and it was very sad to see a young player with such great potential go off the rails like that.

I honestly don't know what my reaction would have been if any player had come to me and told me they were mixed up in heavy duty drugs like that, but I would like to think I would have done my best to help. Colin was one of the crop we took in as we revamped the squad, one of the relatively local lads given their chance to make an impact.

We didn't restrict ourselves to the Scottish market and when it came to replacing Ally Maxwell we cast the net a bit wider. Although Billy Thomson had come into the team and done very well, we knew we needed competition for the No.1 jersey. Ton van Dalen, who had helped us in the past by brokering the deal to bring in Luc Nijoholt, suggested Sieb Dijkstra and we agreed to take him in for a fortnight's trial. I wasn't too keen at all but it was actually Billy, the player who had most to lose by a new keeper coming in, who told me not to be too rash. He thought Sieb had all the attributes to do a good job for us and I backed Billy's judgement on that to sign him. He was absolutely spot on, with Sieb proving a very able shot stopper as well as a strong character.

Rab Shannon came in from Dunfermline, Miodrag Krivokapić from Dundee United as I wanted to add a man marker to the mix, Tommy Coyne from Tranmere and Billy Davies from Dunfermline. Miodrag had been at Tannadice for a couple of years and had done well, but sometimes a staleness can creep in and it is time for a change. Our Jim didn't try and put me off and it was also Jim who put in a good word for Tam Coyne, supporting my own view that he would be good acquisition. I didn't always listen to Jim, but I valued his opinion. There were two or three that I was put off after speaking to him . . . and one in particular that I should have taken his advice on. Paul Kinnaird was that man, someone Jim was quite adamant should be avoided at all costs – he was just a daft laddie and his words to describe him, a bit tongue-in-cheek maybe, were 'stupid-stupid'. He was right, but I didn't listen and signed him anyway. I figured that there was always a risk when you're dealing at the level we were. Jim's verdict? Very much: 'On your head be it.'

Paul had talent, there was no question about that, but he also had issues. Even when I phoned to try and sign him, he had to be pulled out of the bookies to speak to me. That signing didn't pay off, but the vast majority did. It was a process of trying, where possible, to ensure those coming in were of a better quality than those going out to take it to the next level, which was to gain regular European football. It was a long-term project and I knew the direction I wanted to go in. We targeted talented players but they were all good lads into the bargain, honest to goodness 100 per cent types with the correct attitude to their work. The camaraderie was fantastic, but there was hard work ahead.

In the same season we won the Cup, 1990/91, we finished sixth in what was a ten-team Premier Division. It was a comfortable mid-table season, no threat of dipping down to the foot of the table and only eight points off Celtic in third place. Rangers and Aberdeen had fought their battle for the championship, with the trophy going back to Ibrox, but behind them it was very much nip and tuck right the way through. The following season the league was to be expanded, going up to twelve teams, and the expectation levels surrounding Motherwell had grown on the back of the success at Hampden. While I hoped to live up to those, I was also wary of the fact it was a transitional period for us as the new squad began to take shape. It very rarely happens overnight and there was certainly a period of adjustment.

The 1991/92 campaign was another steady one, we sat just outside the top half of the table for the majority of the year but went on a horrible run of five straight defeats in the last five fixtures to end up tenth. Again, relegation wasn't a worry, but the results certainly were. The defence of the Scottish Cup had ended in the fourth round when we were beaten 2–1 by Rangers at Ibrox and we had a very disappointing 4–1 defeat against Raith Rovers in the second round of the League Cup, so the prospects of silverware were dashed early on. Winning a place in the European Cup Winners' Cup had been a fantastic spin-off of our win against Dundee United, but the draw wasn't so welcome. I went out to see the names being pulled from the hat and was sitting beside Walter Smith – he couldn't hide his smiles when we were plucked out alongside Katowice, having been there before. It was, he took great pleasure in telling me, not the ideal destination.

We went out to Poland for the first leg and lost 2–0, leaving us with a mountain to climb, but once again the Motherwell supporters rose to the occasion and the players responded. We won 3–1 at Fir Park with a fantastic performance but the away goal killed us. It finished 3–3 on aggregate but it was Katowice who went through.

The 1992/93 season consisted of more of the same in the Cups – going out 2–0 to Rangers in the third round of the Scottish Cup and 1–0 to Falkirk at the same stage of the League Cup, and to compound matters the league form continued to be bumpy to say the least. By the halfway stage we were rooted to the bottom, but we managed to dig out the results we needed to climb clear of the drop zone. By the final day of the season we had clawed our way up to ninth, six points clear of Falkirk and Airdrie who were tied at the bottom and a point above Dundee in tenth.

It is a results-driven business and past glories count for very little. Cup win or not, I knew we needed a big season to vindicate the decisions I'd taken in rebuilding on the back of the trophy success. When I needed it most, the squad responded in the best way possible.

20

SO NEAR, YET SO FAR

Three games. Just 270 minutes. That is how close Motherwell came to winning the Premier Division championship in 1993/94 and while we fell at the final hurdle, I consider it to be one of the most significant achievements of my career. In so many ways it was the culmination of everything we had set out to achieve, taking a financially stricken club from the First Division to the heights of the top flight with a team that had been built with a mixture of home-grown talent and inexpensive recruits. At the time the pain of not making it across the finish line in first place was severe, but as time passed I came to realise that keeping the title chase alive for as long as we did was an achievement in itself. Rangers came through in the end but they were pushed all the way by us and Aberdeen, going right through to those last few weeks.

To put it in context, the first-choice team at Ibrox that season was Ally Maxwell (£250,000), Gary Stevens (£1m), David Robertson (£1m), Richard Gough (£1.5m), Davie McPherson (£1.3m), Stuart McCall (£1.25m), Trevor Steven (£1.5m), Ian Ferguson (£850,000), Gordon Durie (£1.2m), Mark Hateley (£500,000) and Alexei Mikhailachenko (£2m). There was the luxury of Ally McCoist to call upon when needed too. That made for a combined value of more than £12 million for the starting eleven alone, not taking into account the strength in depth that included the likes of Andy Goram, Ian Durrant, John Brown, Steven Pressley . . . the list goes on.

In contrast we had spent less than £500,000 on our squad, far less than we had taken in through sales. We shouldn't have been in the same ballpark as that Rangers team but we went toe to toe for the vast majority of the season and did it in style. Going into the last three games we were level on points and had everything to play for. We hadn't been beaten in ten games and had defeated Rangers, Celtic and Hibs during that run. In short, the only thing we hadn't done was hit the top of the table.

It was an incredibly tight Premier Division that season and it meant that just about every team had something to play for, compounded by the fact the division was being cut from twelve teams to ten so three were going down. In the case of Dundee United and St Johnstone, two of the sides we had to face in the run in, it was survival that was on the line. They were fighting to stay in the league and every point was a prisoner. Raith Rovers was the third team in our list of closing fixtures and were already relegated, so on paper and, according to the form book, represented the easiest of the three matches. It worked out that way – but not in the way we would have expected. We took a point against Raith at Stark's Park in the middle of our three games, the only one we added to our total from a possible six.

When Dundee United came to Fir Park for the first of that series they left with a 2–1 victory. That, more than any other result, was a shattering blow to our hopes of pipping Rangers to the post. By the time we fell to a 1–0 defeat at home to St Johnstone on the last day of the season it was already over, although it did mean Aberdeen managed to leapfrog us and take the runners-up spot. That was one last kick to the shins after what had been a monumental effort by our players. I was proud of the way they rose to the challenge of taking on the Rangers machine and for their sake it would have been just reward to have lifted the trophy.

When you consider the huge sums of money being invested at Ibrox, that Motherwell team shouldn't have got close, but in my opinion, despite the huge gulf in transfer value and wages, it was every bit as good as the side at Rangers. We had a great blend of steel, creativity, intelligence and spirit. It had taken two years to get to that stage, but it had clicked for us and to see it come to fruition was a satisfying experience for myself and the coaching team.

For any manager it is a lovely feeling to go into every match feeling confident of winning, and that was certainly the way it felt that season. Of course we didn't win them all but we gave ourselves a good chance. We beat Rangers at Ibrox, Celtic home and away, Hearts home and away, Dundee United home and away and Hibs at Easter Road, amongst others. The points-tally was five from a possible eight against Celtic, four from eight against Rangers and four from eight against Aberdeen.

I had enormous faith in the group we had pulled together and they worked hard each and every day on the training field, boosted at various stages when we were able to bring in players to give us a lift at the right time. We set high standards but at the same time were careful not to ask anyone to do things they weren't capable of.

We had led the league early in the campaign for a month or so before being overtaken by Rangers. After around a third of the season we hit the top of the table again and held it for another month before Rangers came back at us. We certainly weren't playing catch-up all the way through, and it gave Walter Smith and everyone at Rangers food for thought – with the nine-in-a-row quest in full flow and the pressure building on them to keep that run going.

As underdogs you might presume we, on the other hand, were free from that weight of expectation. In actual fact, it doesn't matter whether you're red-hot favourites or rank outsiders – if you are in first place, you believe you can win and are desperate to do that. Naturally that brings its own pressure, something we dealt with well. It wasn't nerves that cost us in the end, just the difference in strength in depth between our squad and that at Ibrox when it came to the business end of what had been a long, hard and tiring season.

Through all the drama on the pitch, there was a separate story unfolding behind the scenes that very few people were aware of. I was in the last year of my contract going in to that 1993/94 season and talks began during the course of the campaign with a view to agreeing a new deal. My financial advisor, John Murray, had been doing some work in the background and he was adamant I was the lowest paid manager in the Premier Division as things stood. In his opinion, on the back of the Cup win a couple of seasons earlier and the ongoing challenge for the championship, that was an anomaly that had to be rectified in the new contract. I shared his thoughts on that. I had never been one to go banging on the chairman's door demanding this or that, but the advice I was getting was that it was time to start putting me and my family first and to aim for a contract that reflected the progress we were making. By the same token we weren't asking for a king's ransom, just a reasonable raise to bring me in line with other managers operating at the same level.

While the talks had been opened for a while, it wasn't until the February of 1994 that it began to become strained. John Murray had gone in with his facts and figures hoping to get the ball rolling properly over discussions on terms, but the chairman, John Chapman, didn't see it that way. John was a tremendous chairman but a terrible negotiator. I say that because there was no negotiation. He had his price in mind –whether for a transfer fee or wages – and he wouldn't budge. The only way he would barter was down. It turned out to be exactly the same when it came to my contract, he wasn't in the mood for negotiation and it was frustrating when John and I found ourselves getting nowhere with the talks with the club.

I was keen to stay and finish the job I had started but there had to be a little bit of give and take from the board. I didn't have any thoughts on what else I would do, no Plan B, but I wasn't prepared just to roll over.

Then I got a call out of the blue from a professional headhunting agency. It was all very mysterious, but they wanted to sound me out about the possibility of a vacancy they thought I would be suited to. At that stage I put it in the hands of Jock Brown, who was my lawyer, to find out more. He was happy to do that – I think he enjoyed the intrigue as much as anything. It turned out like something from a film with Jock getting invited to meetings that were still cloak and dagger. All we were told was that the agency was working on behalf of a consortium that was intent on buying a 'major' Scottish club. As part of that they wanted to make their own managerial appointment and I was the man they wanted.

We genuinely didn't know for certain who was involved or which club it was, but through a process of elimination it wasn't too difficult to whittle it down. Hearts was the one that stood out and within a few weeks, after more calls and meetings between Jock and the representatives of the consortium, that proved to be the case. It had been an eventful season for Hearts on and off the park. Before a ball had been kicked, Wallace Mercer had put his shareholding up for sale. He had also sacked Joe Jordan and appointed Sandy Clark to the manager's job, but it had been tough for him to improve fortunes on the field with so much uncertainty in the background. They ended up just outside the top six, just a couple of points clear of relegated St Johnstone.

The steer we were getting from the consortium's representatives was that if their people went ahead with the purchase of the club they wanted a more experienced manager in charge. It wasn't a reflection on Sandy's ability as a coach, simply the direction they wanted to take with the team. They wanted an older head as well as a fresh pair of eyes who didn't have a connection to the club or to the players.

It was interesting to discover during the talks Jock had with them that the going rate for the job was, as John Murray had advised me, far above what I was being paid by Motherwell. The salary on the table at Tynecastle was 50 per cent higher than my top rate at Fir Park. Of course, the offer would be completely worthless if the takeover didn't go through. It transpired that Chris Robinson and Leslie Deans were the men aiming to buy Mercer's shares and it took several months for that to be concluded.

At the same time as Jock was speaking to that group, I was negotiating with Motherwell. It was only right that I handled that side of things as I had a long and good relationship with the board. It went beyond that of employer-employee, as far as I was concerned.

That was why what happened next came as a surprise to me, with a letter landing on my mat from the club's solicitors. It was a take it or leave it offer, representing a small increase in salary but short of what I felt was reasonable. Certainly far short of what Hearts were offering, not that Motherwell were aware of that and nor did I want them to be – I had no interest in trying to play one off against the other, all I wanted was an offer that they and I felt fair.

As soon as the letter arrived I knew that one way or another I would be leaving. It was obvious that they were already being pushed higher than they were comfortable with in terms of wages and I was no longer comfortable operating at the lower level. From both sides, the relationship could never be a strong one from that point on. I have to admit the handling of the situation disappointed me, particularly that letter. It was such a formal and impersonal step to take, and given the length of time I had been at Fir Park and the extent to which I had been involved in all aspects of the club, it was something that could have been done face to face. In fact, it didn't have to be done at all. It could all have been sorted for me to have stayed quite easily. I felt Bill Dickie, who was vice-chairman at that stage, could have exerted more of an influence but he chose to let John Chapman take the lead and events began to snowball from there. The lawyer's letter was a real slap in the face. Having left the Hearts approach in Jock's hands, it was after that final offer from Motherwell that I became involved in those talks.

While all of that was bubbling away behind the scenes, we were pushing hard to win the championship. I can say, hand on heart, that it didn't distract me from the job in hand. With a game every week to focus on that is what consumes your time and your attention regardless of what else is happening in your life. The bottom line was that I was desperate to do my best for Motherwell.

As I said, my first choice would have been to stay at Motherwell but it had become apparent it wouldn't happen. Even without the offer from Hearts, I would have had to have walked away at the end of that season. I had nothing else on the horizon and no thought to what I would do, but it was time for a clean break.

And the more I spoke to Chris Robinson and Leslie Deans, the more enthusiastic I was about the challenge at Tynecastle. I went to meet them at Hopetoun House near Edinburgh and was quite happy with what I was told, with plans for a share issue in the pipeline and what appeared to be solid plans for the club going forward.

Just as it had been in the early days at Motherwell, one of the key objectives from the off was financial – the wage bill was to be lowered substantially. With big earners such as Mo Johnston, Alan McLaren, Craig Levein and John Robertson on the books the new regime was looking at a different business model. I was comfortable with that and felt combining that whilst improving results was achievable. Tough, but not impossible. But again, it all revolved around the deal with Wallace Mercer being struck to allow Robinson and Deans to take control at Hearts. By the time my contract had expired at Motherwell and I cleared my desk, it still had not been concluded.

I went away on holiday that summer not knowing where my future would lie. Of course I'd prepared for taking on the job at Hearts, I had an idea in my own mind how I would approach it, but that was as far as I could go.

While I was away I got a phone call to say the takeover had gone through. It was a sense of relief, excitement and trepidation all rolled into one. After so long at Fir Park it was a wrench to leave and going in to a new environment and to a club under new ownership was going to be a challenge for everyone involved. At that stage in my career I felt I was ready for it.

Back at Motherwell, the wheels were in motion to find my successor and the decision was taken to go in the opposite direction to Hearts. Rather than experience they went for a new face in the shape of Alex McLeish as player-manager. That was a rarity in the Premier Division and a tough role for anyone to take on, but from the club's perspective I imagine it was viewed as a fresh approach. What did baffle me was the fact they had to pay a £30,000 fee to recruit Alex from Aberdeen, having decided they couldn't dip into the coffers to come up with a contract to keep me at the club. I've no idea what sort of terms Alex was on, but with the transfer fee taken into account, I can't imagine the change actually saved the club more money than it would have cost to keep me.

Alex came in and made some changes to the side, too many too soon, in my opinion. He was a young manager looking to make his mark on a team he had inherited and I can understand why he did that, but I honestly feel that if that group of players had been allowed to grow together for longer it would have gone on to even bigger and better things. The following season, with Alex in charge, they did finish second – but were fifteen points behind Rangers. It wasn't as close as it had been previously and from then on the changes began to impact and the challenge faded further.

I admit it was tough for me to watch from the outside, I was proud of what I achieved at Fir Park. I left Motherwell, but Motherwell never left me.

21

CAPITAL CHALLENGE

The debate has raged on for decades around which club can justifiably claim to be Scotland's third force. Aberdeen and Dundee United, at the peak of their powers in the 1980s, would have argued their case and Hibs, going back further in time, too would stake a claim. But in my eyes it is Hearts that truly come closest to matching the Old Firm in terms of potential, support and passion from the fans. That was the big attraction for me when it came to moving to Tynecastle. I had loved playing in Gorgie in my younger years, with the crowd right on top of you and a wonderful atmosphere in the ground.

As a manager taking teams to play Hearts, it was always a venue you relished going to for the same reasons – there never seemed to be a quiet or uneventful game, always lots of excitement and drama. The opportunity to work on the other side of the fence and in that type of environment was fantastic and despite the obvious challenges it didn't frighten me at all.

The first thing I said was that I wanted to keep Walter Kidd on the coaching staff. He was a Hearts man through and through as well as knowing the club and the city inside out. Tam Forsyth followed me across from Motherwell. We knew ourselves inside out and worked well together, so he was a great ally to have. My other appointment was Eammon Bannon, who had been away from Hearts and working with Hibs before I appointed him as a coach shortly after checking in at Tynecastle. With his experience and knowledge of the game he was perfect for the role, as well as having a good feel for the football scene in Edinburgh.

Getting the staff in place was the relatively simple part; it was on the playing side that the real challenge would be in the months ahead. What I knew from the initial discussions I had with the new owners was that the players I brought in would be of lesser quality than those going out – and I mean no disrespect to the signings from that period when I say that. I was working to specific aims in terms of the wage bill and it stands to reason that when you lower the expenditure you have to work in a different market.

The players leaving were internationals, but I couldn't afford to shop at that level. For example, Mo Johnston was moved on to Falkirk and Colin Cramb came in the opposite direction. Colin was a solid Premier Division striker, but his experience didn't compare to that of Maurice. Alan McLaren went to Rangers, a promising young Scotland player. The deal had already been brokered by the time I came in and involved bringing Davie McPherson in the opposite direction, which isn't necessarily the route I would have gone down. In terms of my own signing, it was Willie Jamieson who came in from Partick Thistle as cover – again a good professional, but in a different bracket to the one going out. Tosh McKinlay went out to Celtic, and Colin Millar came in from Hamilton Accies. That was the trend, with players leaving in big moves and others coming in from a lower level. Brian Hamilton was probably the exception, brought in from Hibs, which caused a few grumbles on both sides of the fence.

It quickly became apparent that the funds I had hoped to be available to me simply weren't going to materialise. There were a variety of reasons for that, none I could have any influence on, and I had no option but to accept that and work on as best I could.

The season was a mixed one. In the league it was difficult at times with a team in transition and an understandably expectant crowd. If Hearts are the third force, the supporters are justified in expecting to be challenging for honours every season. We kicked off in the Premier Division with a trip north to face Aberdeen at Pittodrie, far from a gentle start to my time in charge. We lost that game 3–1 and I could see from that match that there was a lot of work to be done to move things forward. We had obviously worked hard in pre-season on fitness and shape, but it is only when the competitive action begins that you get a real sense of where the strengths and weaknesses are in a team and in a squad.

Mind you, the close season hadn't been entirely peaceful in the Hearts camp. One of my first tasks was to deal with the fallout of the infamous bust up between Craig Levein and Graeme Hogg in a friendly against Raith. You want to see fire in the bellies of your players, but that was something I'd never encountered before. The sight of Hogg being stretchered off was horrendous, a real embarrassment for the club. Both he and Levein were also red carded for their troubles. I acted quickly to fine them both the maximum of two weeks' wages and also made both available for transfer. In the end it was Hogg who left, but the whole affair was a distraction we didn't need when we had so much to get through in terms of preparing for the new season.

After losing to Aberdeen in the opener, a 1–0 defeat to Hibs a fortnight later was my first taste of the Edinburgh derby, which was fantastic to be involved in. The result went against us, but the energy from the Tynescastle stands that day was inspiring. When they came to our place later in the season we ran out 2–0 winners, so I did get the opportunity to savour being on the winning side in what is a really special fixture.

That was one of the highlights of the league campaign. Although it was a very frustrating season all round, there were some memorable moments peppered throughout it. We also beat Celtic, Rangers, Aberdeen, Dundee United and Motherwell at home – all traditionally difficult fixtures. We went to Parkhead and won there too, so it wasn't a case of not turning up for the big events – our undoing was too many draws and defeats in matches we would have been expected to win.

At the final count, we were sixth and, crucially, three places beneath Hibs. In the circumstances it was reasonable and represented an improvement on the previous season, despite a major reduction in the wage bill, but it was not in line with what I had hoped for when I took on the job.

The Cup form was what gave hope for the future, with glimpses of what could be possible. In the Scottish Cup we went past Clydebank after a replay in the third round and few gave us much of a chance when we were drawn to play Rangers in the next tie. The performance at Tynecastle, against Walter Smith's team, was superb and we came away with a 4–2 win that sent out a signal of what was possible when it all fell into place.

It was a Monday night game in Edinburgh and the ground was swaying, real spine-tingling stuff. Colin Miller, with a long-range free kick, and Davie McPherson, with a header from close in, put us two ahead before the interval, but Brian Laudrup and Gordon Durie levelled it in the second half. I thought then we would struggle to go again, but the boys dug deep and John Robertson, as he had been so many times in front of his crowd, was the hero. He scored a typical Robbo goal to put us 3–2 ahead, reacting first inside the box to tuck home a rebound and catching the Rangers defence flat-footed. We still had to see out half an hour and stood firm in the face of a predictable onslaught, but with the seconds running down we caught them on the break and wrapped up a 4–2 victory. It was an incredible run from deep from Davie McPherson that set it up, making his way into the box and setting up Kevin Thomas perfectly. It was a big night for big Davie, who had been given a rough ride at Ibrox before moving back to Hearts.

It was a brilliant performance, full of spirit and not short of skill either. I wasn't fooled about the work that still needed to be done in freshening up the squad – we had six players over thirty in that team, including Jim Bett at thirty-five – but it was heartening all the same.

Having played the champions in the fourth round, we went on to face the cup holders in the quarter-finals in the shape of Dundee United. Again, the players did everything I asked of them and we came away with a 2–1 victory at home to book our place in the semi-finals. It hadn't looked like being our day when Sergio Gomes put United ahead just a few minutes after the kick-off, but again we showed real character. John Millar, brought in on a free transfer from Blackburn by Joe Jordan, stole the show, scoring twice before the break to give us what proved to be a decisive lead.

I wasn't quite sure how to feel about the draw in the last four of the competition – Hearts v Airdie. McLean v MacDonald. My old pal Doddie had done a fantastic job on a shoestring at Airdrie and had put together a team that was difficult to beat and a real threat to anyone they faced. They were sharp, well drilled and couldn't be taken lightly even if they were playing First Division football at that stage.

Going into the game at Hampden we had injury problems to contend with, not helped by Kevin Thomas declaring himself fit and then breaking down after coming on as a sub. That was a huge blow and a big disappointment in such an important match. We lost 1–0 and it ranks as one of my biggest disappointments in football. Stevie Cooper scored midway through the first half for them and after that we just couldn't break them down. John Robertson was sent off with seconds to go, with frustration starting to get the better of us.

Had we gone through to the final I knew as well as anyone that anything was possible – and a Cup win would have put a completely different perspective on that season for Hearts. Rather than a disappointment, it would have been a success and those ninety minutes against Airdrie proved to be the thinnest of dividing lines. Doddie and his team took their place in the final against Celtic and did themselves proud, just losing out by a single goal. I would have loved to have seen Doddie get his hands on that trophy. After the miracles he worked at Airdrie over the years it would have been the icing on the cake.

Of course, I would have far preferred it to be Hearts out there in the final. It is a great club, it just needs the stability in all areas to be able to fulfil its potential. I can say with sincerity that I hope, for the sake of the supporters, one day soon that happens for them.

22

A FAMILY AFFAIR

The 1994/95 season proved to be my first and last as Hearts manager. I felt very early on that it was not the right job for me, with the failure of the share issue to reach the target level anticipated as well as other costs that the new board encountered after the takeover. There were also rumours of a split between the new owners Chris Robinson and Leslie Deans. I was left frustrated and disappointed that my plans for the future of the club could not be fulfilled, and had suggested at several stages during the season that if we could reach an amicable agreement we could go our separate ways.

That was behind the scenes, but in July 1995 the club issued a statement explaining that I had asked to be released from my contract during that campaign and that they were now willing to offer me a settlement to end my tenure. I had spoken to Jock Brown, who was still representing me, about the possibility of leaving but it wasn't until the season drew to a close, with Hearts safely in the Premier Division, that there was movement. The statement in July had stated the club's position. Although I left the job at that point, the mechanics didn't prove as straightforward as perhaps the comments in the press suggested.

We failed to agree a settlement figure for the remainder of my contract and it resulted in a long and drawn-out legal dispute. That ended in court in 1996, but until then I had been kicking my heels waiting for a conclusion. It was difficult for me, having never been out of football for more than a few weeks in all my adult life. There may have been an expectation on the part of Hearts that another job would crop up for me while we waited for a court date to be issued, which would have brought the issue to an end.

It was scheduled for three days and evidence was led, but while all of that was going on there was a bizarre twist. With the solicitors doing battle in their natural environment, I was offered the chance to get back to my own favourite place – the training field. Raith Rovers made an approach during the court hearing and I arranged to meet Alex Penman, who was the chairman at that stage, and Willie Gray, the metal dealer who went on to have an involvement with East Fife. I went and met with them at the hotel on the north side of the Forth Road Bridge and was excited by the prospect of getting back to work. That twist led us to conclude the court case early, settling on compensation for the remainder of my Hearts contract to everyone's satisfaction. It opened the door for me to move to Raith Rovers and I was confirmed as the new boss at Stark's Park on 3 September 1996. What I didn't realise and that nobody could have possibly predicted was how short my time with Raith would be. But more on that later.

The job I was hired to do in Fife was to try and salvage the season for the club. Jimmy Thomson had lost his job after a miserable start to the Premier Division season and just a few weeks into the campaign, the directors were already getting nervous about staying in the Premier Division. It was a chance for me to get back to work on the frontline, which was important, and I was confident I could turn things around.

It was after the phenomenal success Jimmy Nicholl had enjoyed with Raith, so there weren't the direct comparisons between the existing team and the heroes of the not too distant past. There were experienced and influential players on the books at the time, including Jim McInally and my old Motherwell striker Stevie Kirk. They were going to have to help lift the spirits because the confidence had ebbed away, even in the short period from the start of the season to the time of my own appointment.

Jimmy Thomson had been in charge of the youth set-up under Jimmy Nicholl. When Nicholl moved to Millwall and took his assistant Martin Harvey with him, the board turned to Jimmy Thomson to take charge. He had fulfilled his part of the bargain by steadying the ship at a time when a number of players from the successful team under Jimmy Nicholl were getting itchy feet. After the change in manager, more than £1.5 million in transfer fees had been raked in and there had been a decent amount of money reinvested in the squad.

At the end of the 1995/96 season it was mission accomplished for Jimmy Thomson, with Raith finishing sixth in the table and well clear of relegation. Improving on that would have been the aim but the next season had started with a 1–0 defeat away to Rangers, a 4–1 thumping at Celtic and 3–0 loss at home to Motherwell in the league. A 3–2 defeat against Airdrie in the League Cup had added to that run and after those four results the decision was made by the board to make a change.

There were plenty of names being bandied around in the press at the time. Jim McInally had been serving as Jimmy Thomson's assistant and was one being mentioned as a possible successor, with others including Willie Miller and Steve Archibald, as well as John Brown at Rangers. With the exception of Willie, none had managed in the Premier Division and that would have represented a gamble. Instead the directors opted for experience and when I spoke to them I was impressed by what they had to say.

The timing coincided with a break in the league fixtures, giving them the opportunity to make an appointment in time for the next game, which was another potentially tough encounter with Aberdeen at Stark's Park. After my appointment was confirmed, I had a few days to get to grips with the job ahead and get to know the squad as we prepared for that match against the Dons. I had hoped for a lift from my arrival, the usual new manager bounce. If I got it, I certainly didn't see it reflected in the score line – we went down 4–1 and I knew at the end of those ninety minutes that it would be a rocky path to safety.

The loss of a lot of key players – the likes of Jason Dair, Paul Hartley and Stevie Crawford – had taken its toll on the team. Creativity was an issue and the rate at which goals were being leaked was obviously a huge concern. I hadn't been promised a pot of gold to spend, so it was always going to be a case of tweaking what we had and working with the players already on the books.

The first game was disappointing, and I also took a reserve team north to play Aberdeen at Cove as I began to make my mind up about the way we had to go, similar to the process I'd gone through in the early days at Hearts. The difference at Raith was that it was a rescue job rather than a long-term project, in the first instance at least. Survival was the key in that first season and there was ground to be made up on those further up the table. In the previous season, after winning promotion they had finished comfortably mid-table but the tricky second season is always the most difficult for any team that comes up. The adrenalin and buzz of being back in the top flight has worn off by then and the other teams have also started to get the measure of you.

Raith had started the season at the foot of the table without a point, and with some tricky fixtures lined up ahead, it was important to get off the mark quickly and avoid becoming detached from the rest of the pack just above us. That pack included Dundee United, who had come back into the Premier Division after a year down in the First Division. Billy Kirkwood had taken them up through the play-offs, but it had been a sticky season for them out of the top flight. Certainly not the walk in the park many had expected. They huffed and puffed and got there in the end.

Billy had done what he had set out to do in winning promotion, but it wasn't in the style that the supporters would have liked. Getting off to a good start back in the big league was imperative to settle the nerves, but it didn't happen. A single point from the first four games was a disappointing tally and it was only the even worse form of Raith that had kept them off the foot of the table.

It was a League Cup tie against Dundee at Tannadice at the start of September that proved to be the final straw. United lost on penalties after a 2–2 draw at the end of extra-time and it set alarm bells ringing. Billy was removed from his post and I got a call that I hadn't expected – it was our Jim, phoning to ask if I would be interested in the manager's job at Tannadice. I was a week into my new job at Raith, really content to be back in among it, and then I was hit with that.

The honest answer to an honest question was 'yes'. Of course I was interested. Regardless of what people looking in from the outside might have said about it and about the ethics of it happening so soon after I had agreed to take over at Raith, it is impossible to cast judgement until you have been in that situation. My big brother, chairman of the club he had poured so much of his time and energy into, had come to me to ask for my help. Even if I had refused to let my heart rule my head I would have come to the conclusion that the United job was a better fit for me at that stage of my career. It was a club with great potential and one with ambitions of doing more than simply surviving from year to year in that division. The goal was to be challenging for honours and that was a massive draw to me. I had been out of the game for more than a year at that point and was desperate to make up for lost time.

After the initial approach from Jim, I called Jock Brown to ask his advice. He summed up the situation in two words: 'Bloody hell.' Jock had not long finished tying up the loose ends with Raith Rovers, now I was asking him to look at getting me out of the same contract. But it was Jock who was the most objective person in the whole affair. Simply put, he asked me who I felt offered the best chance of success. The answer to that was the answer to where my future would lie.

There were various options put in front of me. I could have walked out and left Raith to pursue me for the week's wages I had been paid. But I wasn't hoping for a shortcut, and neither were Dundee United, to give them their credit. Jim was adamant he wanted to do things properly and offered to pay them the equivalent of my annual salary at Raith to buy out my contract. Had the board come to the same conclusion just a couple of weeks earlier, before I had gone through with the move to Kirkcaldy, he could have saved his club a decent sum of money, but he was desperate to see Billy succeed in the manager's job. He'd had him under his wing as a player during great times in the 1980s and had seen him blossom into a fine coach. The directors stuck by him during a tough season in the First Division and had been reluctant to make the change, but they decided they had to bring in experience to the manager's office. What I wanted to know was that it was a unanimous decision by the board, rather than something Jim was driving. I was given that assurance, which gave me the peace of mind I needed.

I stuck with my usual philosophy of offering the existing staff the chance to stay on, and that included Billy Kirkwood. I would have been delighted if he had stayed on in a coaching capacity, but I understood why he opted for a clean break. It would have been hard to take that step back, but I genuinely believed it could have worked. It had been similar at Raith, where Jimmy Thomson had been offered the chance by the board to go back to his youth role after being replaced as manager, but he too preferred to step away.

They had their decisions to make and I had mine too when it came to whether or not to make the switch to Tannadice. To be fair, the major concern in my mind was for Jim rather than for myself. The worry was what would happen if it didn't work out as we hoped, if performances on the park didn't meet expectations. At the end of the day, like I've said before, football is a results-driven business and there was the possibility that as my employer he could have been put in a very difficult position.

The solution, quite simply, was that if either of us had any issue with the way things were going we could voice them early and voice them clearly. If there was any doubt at all, we would go our separate ways and we would do it amicably. We went into the working relationship with no grey areas.

It wasn't quite so amicable back in Fife, where Alex Penman kicked up hell. I was being slaughtered left, right and centre for walking away, and I understood why feelings were running so high. I couldn't let that cloud my judgement and had to press on with the decision I felt was right for me. Poor old Jock was very much the man stuck in the middle, but he managed to iron things out in the end. He earned his fees with that one.

I'd recommended Iain Munro as my successor, with Iain doing a very good job at Hamilton. He was appointed to the Raith post but it proved to be an impossible job and they went down at the end of the season, having won just nine games in the whole campaign.

Obviously I kept an eye out for the Raith results, but I didn't have time to look back. The job at United was a big one and I threw my heart and soul into it. At Raith I was intending to commute across from Larkhall, but Dundee United was a different animal and I knew I needed to be close to the club. For the first time in our lives, Beth and I decided to uproot and head for pastures new in Dundee. The club had been quite clear that the manager's job would require me to be based near to Tannadice and it had always been the same policy with players too, with a determination to foster a spirit of togetherness and ensure the connection to the city and the club extended beyond the pay packet.

When I got in and had a close look at the players on the books, I wasn't disappointed. There was a good solid base to build on at Tannadice, although I did feel there were a few immediate adjustments to be made that would make a real difference to the way the results were going. One of the key ones was to bring Maurice Malpas into the centre of the defence to play in a sweeper-type role, the free man behind two markers in Steven Pressley and Mark Perry. Elvis had been operating as the free man prior to that, but I felt the experience of Maurice would do that job more justice.

There were other old heads in the squad to help the cause, with Davie Bowman adding tenacity and skill to the midfield. Gary McSwegan was another who had experience and was always liable to score a goal or two whilst Robbie Winters, though still young, was showing the type of potential that, when mated to his pace, was really catching the eye. The enigma that was Andy McLaren was also on the books, someone I was determined to get the best out of by hook or by crook. Andy was a real talent but so terribly unpredictable, obviously blighted by problems off the park but none of us were aware at that stage the extent of those demons. The revelations later in his career about drug use were a complete shock, but it was encouraging to see him finally confront the issues that had blighted his career and try to put things right.

While working with Andy was frustrating, it was a similar position to that I had been in throughout my managerial career – to paraphrase the late Willie Waddell, I had to work with what I had. Again there wasn't an open chequebook, but I was still able to bring in players to strengthen the squad. My first port of call was Stark's Park – something that didn't improve relations between the two clubs particularly. I went back to sign Jim McInally and offered what I thought was a reasonable fee, with the player given permission to speak to us. Then Raith changed their mind and asked for an extra slice of cash to push the deal through. After batting things back and forth, we eventually struck a deal and Jim was delighted to be on his way back to Tannadice. Even in the short time I'd been at Raith, I'd seen enough to know that he could still do a turn. I also wanted him to lend his experience as part of the coaching set-up and he had the authority and stature to make a big impact.

My first game in charge was at home to Celtic, a match we lost 2–1. When we lost 3–2 to Raith at Stark's Park the following week it left us down at the foot of the table for the first time that season. To say the home supporters in Kirkcaldy enjoyed that moment is an understatement – I got a fiery reception and the game was just as tousy, with nothing between the teams. It could easily have gone our way but it didn't and we were left staring up at nine teams above us. It was sink or swim time.

What happened next was every manager's dream. We made progress in small steps to begin with, picking up significant wins against the likes of Aberdeen, Rangers and Hearts, and by Christmas 1996 we had clawed our way up to sixth spot and were in touching distance of the top half of the table. After those small steps came the huge leaps forward. From our 2–0 win against Motherwell at Tannadice on Boxing Day right through to a matching defeat away to Hibs at the start of April we went on a seventeen-game unbeaten run – including fourteen wins within that incredible run of fixtures in the league and Scottish Cup. Our new recruits had been a major influence on the upturn in fortunes, and as I'd done previously at Motherwell, it was overseas that we turned our attention to when we started looking for cost-effective ways of bolstering the squad.

Scandinavia was the market of choice, a good source of technically sound players with reasonable fees and wages that for Scottish clubs were not out of the question. We worked with a Scandinavian agent to identify available players and ploughed through his recommendations. Swedish forward Kjell Olofsson was among those and proved to be the best of a very good crop of players, although there was a touch of fortune in Kjell's move to Scotland.

We were over in Norway looking at various players when his team, Moss, were beaten in the play-offs. That result changed Kjell's situation and in an instant the agent clicked that he might be available. That proved to be the case and we invited Kjell over for a brief trial period – although within the first training session I'd seen enough to decide we had to have him. I remember turning to Jim and saying, 'I think we've won a watch here.' We paid £400,000 but it was money well spent; the goals Kjell scored for the club over the years were worth far more than that. He established himself as a real hero to the supporters, with power and precision in a great striking package.

Lars Zetterland, another Swede, came in at the same time as Kjell and was another hit. Lars was an experienced campaigner and although he didn't score as many goals as I would have liked or expected, he was effective nonetheless. He was a bit of a bonus signing – I hadn't set out to bring him in but spotted him after I'd actually gone out to watch the old Arsenal player Siggi Jonsson, an Icelander, in match action. I'd had a whisper that Siggi might be available, but I found myself just as interested in Lars, and it all rolled on from there. It was a good bit of business for United – not quite two for the price of one, but we signed Jonsson into the bargain.

Erik Pedersen, from Norway, came in at the same time as Kjell, as part of the Scandinavian invasion. Erik was a really good man-marker, capable of sticking to the task with dogged determination and with the intelligence to stay one step ahead. I would use him to cancel out the likes of Paul Gascoigne or Brian Laudrup, but the beauty of Erik was he could also play the game when he was in possession. He was a fantastic midfielder and, in common with the others who came in from that part of the world, a really wonderful professional.

Lars Zetterlund, another Swede, came in around six weeks later and was another hit. Lars was an experienced campaigner and although he didn't score as many goals as I would have liked or expected, he was effective nonetheless. He was a bit of a bonus signing – I hadn't set out to bring him in but spotted him after I'd actually honed in to watch Siggi Jonsson, an Icelander, in another match. I'd had a whisper that Siggi might be available, but I found myself just as interested in Lars, and it rolled on from there. It was a good bit of business for United.

I also brought in Sieb Dijkstra from QPR that season, knowing all about his ability from our time together at Motherwell, and Siggi Jonsson eventually followed in the next campaign.

The great thing about those coming in from Scandinavia was that they settled quickly and embraced not only the football but also the way of life in Scotland. We talk so often of changing our game to fit a more continental approach, but sometimes we also forget that players who want to earn a living here have to adapt too and meet their club and the supporters halfway. The Scandinavians were comfortable socialising with the Scottish lads but knew when to get the serious head on and put the hours in on the training field. I really couldn't have asked for any more from any of them, they ticked all the boxes for me.

I believe Erik left Scotland when he finally departed with a lasting memento, getting a large Dundee United tattoo to serve as a permanent reminder of his time in tangerine. He was a big character and his arrival, along with Kjell and Lars in the autumn, gave us a lift at the right time and helped us kick on. Even now, almost twenty years on, they are well thought of on Tayside and always get a very warm welcome whenever they venture back to Tannadice for occasional visits to their old stomping ground in Dundee. They became real cult heroes. It was all about providing the right balance right the way through the team and with the fresh faces we were getting that, although it was not all one-way traffic, with David Hannah sold to Celtic for £650,000 at the turn of the year to cover the investment we had made in the foreign signings.

The run we went on was unbelievable, it was something no other provincial club had done before or since. With every week the confidence grew and you get to the stage where you feel invincible, which in itself can become dangerous. As a manager the job is to keep the focus every day in training and every time the players cross the line to play a game. We did that for months on end and when the unbeaten streak did come to an end it was a jolt to the system, albeit we knew it would happen at some point. Given this was a team that had been stuck at the bottom of the table, it was an incredible turnaround and I was very impressed by the response I got from the squad as well as the impact the new signings made.

As much as anything, I was pleased for Jim – he and the board had put their necks on the line by appointing me. It certainly wasn't the easy option. I got stick, he got stick and so did the club because of a combination of the situation with Raith Rovers and the accusations of nepotism levelled at Jim for giving his wee brother the job. What I can say is that he let me get on with that job without interference, certainly in a negative sense at least. The only problem I had was his determination to see me succeed, quite often on a Monday he'd come looking for me to see which player I wanted to sign. He knew that was my day for making my moves, my fishing day, and was always willing to back me in the transfer market, desperate to see the improvement continue and buoyed by the good run of form we had been on. It was a role reversal in the traditional manager-chairman relationship, where usually it is the chairman trying to urge caution.

That I could cope with. Had there been any other type of interference I wouldn't have been able to do the job. But we were both singing from the same hymn sheet – we saw the value in stability. There was no question that Jim in many ways had been the problem and he was also the cure. Simply put, it was impossible for those who had followed in his footsteps to live up to the standards he had set, similar to the thankless task for those going after Alex Ferguson at Aberdeen. Ivan Golac and Billy Kirkwood had both tried but there had been turbulent times, but there was a real thirst for continuity in the wake of those appointments and it looked as though my appointment would give them that. I picked up three Manager of the Month awards on the trot, a reflection of the efforts of the team at that stage but also a welcome boost for me after my period out of the game. I never lost belief in my ability or my hunger to win football matches, but I still felt as though I had to prove myself all over again.

I wanted the same continuity on the park as the board wanted off it and the team virtually picked itself during the run in that first season, taking us up to third place by the halfway point and keeping us there, tucked in behind the Old Firm, right through to the end of the season.

In the Scottish Cup too we stayed strong, skipping past Stirling Albion with a 2–0 win in our first tie to set up a fourth-round match against Hearts at Tynecastle. A 1–1 draw took it back to Tannadice for a replay, where we won 1–0. The quarter-final pitted us against Motherwell and we made light work of that one, earning a 4–1 victory, to set up a semi-final against Kilmarnock. I thought we had a really good chance of making the final and on paper we were the favourites, although Killie were having a decent Premier Division season and were a quality team under Bobby Williamson.

Our only major weakness was a thinner squad than I would have liked. We couldn't look to the bench for really top quality reinforcements if we needed to change a game. The initial semi-final finished locked at 0–0, with neither side giving an inch, and by the time we played the replay the other match had been played – Falkirk had beaten Celtic, so we knew who was waiting for the winner of our tie. I'm not sure if that was a blessing or a curse. Certainly both we and Kilmarnock would have fancied our chances of beating Falkirk in a one-off game, so it should have been an incentive. The flip side is it may also have been a distraction.

Either way, we didn't shine on the day of the replay. Kilmarnock came through to win 1–0 and it was a huge disappointment – if we could have made it through the last four and gone on to win the Cup it would have been the perfect season. The replay had gone into extra-time and Jim McIntyre had scored the winner just three minutes before the end of the 120 minutes. I sensed a lifelessness creeping in to our team, the result of a long and gruelling season in which they had been pushing themselves every week to improve and keep the good league form going.

23

TRANSFER TANGLE

The 1996/97 season was notable for me because it marked my return to management. For the game, it was important for a reason more far-reaching than that. It was the era of Jean-Marc Bosman. When Bosman won his case in the European Court of Justice at the tail end of 1995, I don't think he or anyone connected with the sport truly appreciated the repercussions. From a player's point of view, I understood his passion for the cause. I had been in the situation myself as a young man, where I was frustrated by the obstacles in my way when I wanted to better myself but wasn't in control of my own destiny. But as someone with a love of football, I could also see the bigger picture. What the Bosman ruling threatened to do was cut off the life support for clubs up and down the country. The introduction was rushed and not properly thought through, in my opinion.

At Motherwell we had saved the club from terrible consequences by selling wisely and rearing our own crop of young players who in time proved to be valuable assets. We didn't stand in their way when it was time for the next stage in their development, but we were properly compensated through guaranteed transfer fees when that moment came. Dundee United had operated the same model very successfully, able to cherry pick which players would be sold and reinvesting the

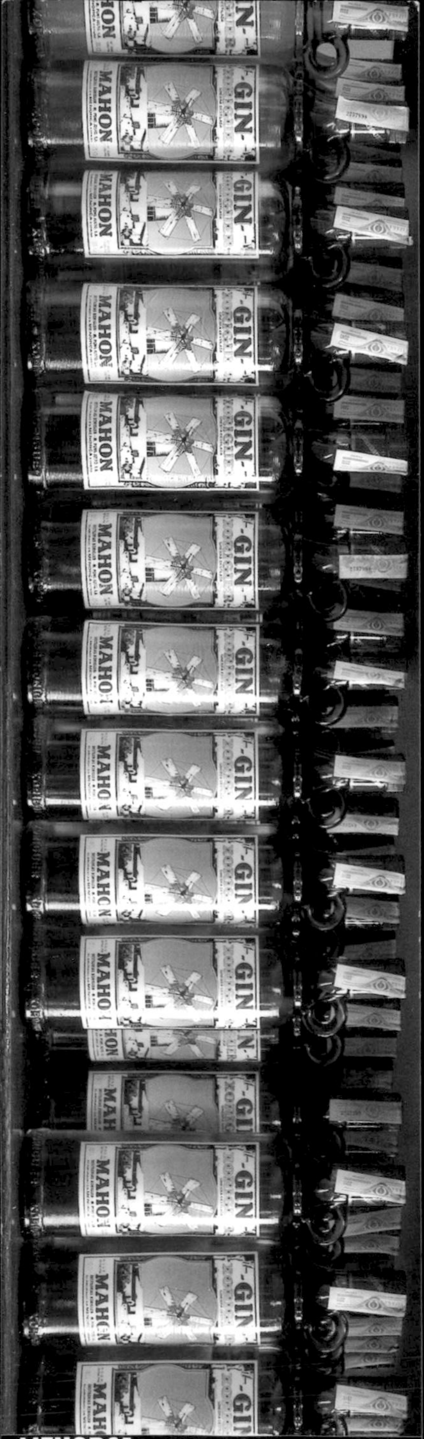

MENORCA
GIN XORIGUER

proceeds to retain the remaining squad members for the long term. It worked.

And then along came Mr Bosman and all of a sudden the manual was ripped up. The first full season of the Bosman ruling was 1996/97, and while we all understood the premise of the new regulations, what we didn't appreciate was how the theory would translate into practice. Sharp practice in many cases.

For Dundee United during my time in charge, two cases in particular illustrated the huge drawbacks of the rules from the perspective of the club and of a manager. The first was Steven Pressley, who had been signed for £750,000 from Coventry City in 1995 as part of the push by Billy Kirkwood to get back to the Premier Division at the first time of asking. Three years later he walked away and joined Hearts on a Bosman free transfer and that £750,000 investment was wiped out in an instant. The negotiations to try and retain Steven were handled by the director, Bill Littlejohn. I was in the room when Bill sat him down and asked: 'Is there anything more that Dundee United can do to make you stay?'

The answer from the player was, 'No, I want to try something different – I want to go abroad.'

That was on the Friday. By Monday he had signed for Hearts and was heading for the sunny climes of Edinburgh.

Mark Perry was another who took advantage of moving on a Bosman, joining Aberdeen in 1998 at the end of his contract. His was a different situation completely, as he hadn't cost Dundee United a transfer fee in the first place, but he had come through the youth system and benefited from the schooling he'd had in football at Tannadice. Then he was gone, without a penny of compensation.

I can remember sitting at the start of pre-season, ready to go, and there being no sign of Mark. I spoke to his agent, Jim

McArthur, and asked what the score was. I was told, 'He's not coming back.' And that was that, no phone call to explain from Mark. Jim promised me he'd get the player to make contact so we could part on decent terms, but it didn't happen. Only silence.

Of course, there were plenty of others who went on their way too, including Pedersen and Olofsson when their contracts expired in the fullness of time, but by that stage we knew that was the likely outcome. With the earlier players it was the manner as much as the financial impact of the moves that caused the most distress. It was rammed home to us that we were in the lap of the gods and the goalposts had shifted completely. The root of the problem was that the players and their agents didn't really know how to deal with the newfound freedom. Rather than being open and honest, there was a whole cloak-and-dagger act creeping in.

In time everyone began to understand that secrecy didn't actually aid negotiation. It was far better for the player if their existing club knew they had competition while they were still in a position to make a counter offer. Early doors the opposite appeared to be the prime tactic employed, with the club always the last to know what was happening with the departing player.

Regardless of the ethics or the protocol being employed, the outcome was the most hurtful part of it all. Transfer income plummeted, wages crept up as the power swung firmly in favour of the players and their agents, and the majority of clubs simply weren't equipped to plug the gap in finances that Bosman created. Nearly twenty years on, Scottish football is still feeling the pain.

Some clubs have coped better than others – Hibs have reinvented the 'selling club' model in a very profitable manner and Dundee United, to an extent, have profited from moving on the players produced through the youth system. Others, for example Aberdeen, have rarely been able to command the type of significant transfer fees that in the pre-Bosman era were the lifeblood of the club. It represents progress in many ways, but at a heavy price.

24

ONWARDS AND UPWARDS

After the honeymoon of my first season at Tannadice, the second year was always going to be a huge challenge. The encouraging thing going into that campaign was the support I had from the directors of Dundee United. That was borne out before a ball had been kicked in 1997/98, when the vice-chairman Doug Smith sought me out and did something that was totally unique to me in football management. Without prompting, Doug told me he wanted to offer me a pay rise as part of a revised contract to mark the achievements of my first season. It was a wonderful gesture, a genuine vote of confidence in the work that was being done.

We had finished third in the previous season and reached the Scottish Cup semi-final. Bettering that was going to be difficult, but we felt it was possible. Whilst our league placing slipped – we finished seventh – we did manage to go one better in the knock-out competitions and reached the final of the League Cup. That certainly ticked one box, as the supporters were craving that type of big occasion, having been brought up on a diet of regular success.

The huge regret I have from my time on Tayside is that we simply didn't deliver when it came to the crunch, freezing on the day of the final against Celtic. The game, played at Ibrox because of the reconstruction work at Hampden, was a fantastic opportunity but we didn't take it. I don't have any great explanation or big excuse – we simply didn't turn up on the day and our reward for that was a 3–0 defeat. Celtic won at a canter.

The build-up had gone to plan. We'd stayed down at the Crowne Plaza on the eve of the game, everything was set as we had hoped and the team ready to go. Celtic were on the up under Wim Jansen and had a trump card in the shape of Henrik Larsson, who was finding his feet in Scotland but already showing signs of the shape of things to come. It was Jansen's first season and there was no doubt there had been a big bounce for the team and the club, something we'd seen at first hand just the week before the Cup final when we'd gone to Parkhead in the league and been beaten 4–0.

That was a sore one to take, but I honestly didn't fear anything similar in the Cup. We should have had enough in our locker to handle them, but a disappointing opening to the game cost us dearly. Inside twenty-five minutes we were two behind, with Marc Rieper and Larsson doing the damage. Both were avoidable goals, in my opinion, but we made it easy for them.

We rallied in the second half, at least forcing a couple of chances, but when Craig Burley scored with a header on the hour mark we knew it was all over for us. Morten Wieghorst was a powerhouse for them and we weren't at the races. There was nothing I would have changed about the preparation or the way we set ourselves up for that match.

Having done so much good work on the run to the final, it was a shame to go out with a whimper. We had come in at the second-round stage and beat Queen of the South 4–2 to set up a tie against Hibs. It took extra-time, but we defeated them 2–1 in the end. We got into the habit of leaving things late, needing extra time again when we tackled Rangers. This time it was the only goal of the game that settled it, with Gary McSwegan doing the business. The semi-final was against Aberdeen, so the draw couldn't have been any tougher. When we defeated them 3–1 to set up the Cup final appearance, I was overjoyed. I thought we had a really good chance.

Celtic later put us out of the Scottish Cup that season, beating us 3–2 at Tannadice, and seemed to hold the Indian sign over us, and it proved to be of those years in which everything was so near yet so far. Obviously we had the joy of reaching the Cup final and the despair of losing it, and in Europe it was a similar experience.

In the UEFA Cup we drew CE Principat of Andorra in the first qualifying round, having the honour of providing the opposition for their first ever tie in European football. There was an element of going into the unknown, but we knew it should have been a formality against what was a part-time team from a tiny principality. Both ties were played before the Scottish season had kicked-off, so it was part of our pre-season in effect, and an 8–0 win in Andorra followed by a 9–0 victory back on Tayside was just what the doctor ordered as we prepared for the domestic competition.

The second qualifying round took us to Turkey to face Trabzonspor, where the atmosphere was everything you would expect. The Turkish fans have a reputation for intimidation, but what they also have is an incredible passion for their teams and we had to try and shut that out and do our own thing. That proved to be easier said than done, with flares, firecrackers and, at one point, even gunfire echoing around a ground that was undergoing reconstruction. Because of the building work the capacity had been restricted to 16,000, but it was still bedlam inside the stadium.

Before a ball had been kicked we knew not to expect a level

playing field. When we had turned up for our obligatory training session on the home pitch on the eve of the tie we found there were no footballs in sight. The home team is required to provide those, but Trabzonspor chose to ignore that and did their best to disrupt us. I took the players up into the stand and said we would sit there as long as it took for them to get things sorted – all night if we had to. Sure enough, they produced the balls that they couldn't seem to find a few minutes earlier.

The game itself was just as fiery as the build-up. All of the talk pre-match had been about Abdullah Ercan – or Abdullah the Mighty, as he was known in the Turkish press. Chelsea were said to be ready to pay £3 million for him but on the night he was quiet, it was his Turkey teammate Hami who ran the show for them.

We defended resolutely, with Sieb Dijkstra certainly earning his money that evening, and were so close to coming away with a draw. It took a penalty in the seventy-sixth minute, tucked away by Hami, to give them the lead the home support was baying for. We'd lost 5–1 to Rangers before we went into the second leg and made big changes to the team to face Trabzonspor, although the reality is that wasn't a kneejerk reaction to the Ibrox performance, as it was always going to be a different approach for the UEFA Cup tie.

The reshuffle worked, with Andy McLaren scoring with a great header after the break to put us one up on the night and level the tie at 1–1. We hammered them in terms of possession and chances but were hit with a real sucker punch just nine minutes from time when Hami popped up again to score. That was enough to give them a 1–1 draw at Tannadice and a 2–1 aggregate win, a real injustice on the balance of play, in my opinion. It was typical of the breaks that went against us throughout the months that unfolded from there. We ended up seventh in the table after mixed form in the league, but with a little touch of good fortune we could have finished in the top half of the table, with a decent European run under our belt and the League Cup on the sideboard. The dividing line is always a thin one to tread.

Going in to the 1998/99 season it was clear change was needed, the squad needed freshened up. There was no question of being content with what we already had, either on my part or that of the board. There wasn't a huge budget to work with, so we had to try and do things differently. The Scandinavian recruits had given great service, but that was a market that had caught up with the rest of Europe and we were finding ourselves being priced out. Instead we were looking further afield and were working with South American agents, including Marcelo Houseman. Marcelo is the brother of Rene Houseman, the former Argentine international, and was very well connected. He had worked with Jim in the past and it had been an effective partnership, but unfortunately for me it was slim pickings by the time I was introduced to him. Marcelo began sending over players that simply weren't up to the standard we required and certainly not the ones we had picked out ourselves or were expecting to arrive.

That had an impact on morale for the players who we already had on the books, to see a succession of trialists coming in that were, in all honesty, poor players. I hold my hands up to that; there were too many coming in and it was a distraction. The bottom line was that we had to be inventive in the transfer market. It was a necessity rather than a choice.

Signing Jean-Jacques Missé, better known simply as Missé-Missé, from Trabzonspor at the start of 1998 was an example of that. I'd been impressed by what I'd seen of him in the UEFA Cup tie against us, and when I heard there were problems in

Turkey and that wages weren't being paid we nipped in to sign him on a free transfer. He was desperate to cement his place in the Cameroon squad for the World Cup that summer, so that rather than big money was the motivation from his side.

That was very much a short-term fix to try and add some spark going into the second half of 1997/98, but for the following campaign we wanted longer-term solutions. I had signing targets in mind and set about strengthening behind the scenes too, with the appointment of Terry Butcher to the coaching staff during the build-up to the 1998/99 kick-off. Big Terry had taken some blows during his time as a manager but he kept coming back fighting. He had been working with Raith Rovers when I approached him to move to Tannadice and he fitted in perfectly, hitting it off straight away with Maurice Malpas. The pair of them worked so well together and it has been no surprise to me to see how that partnership has blossomed, first of all at Motherwell and more recently with the success they have enjoyed in Inverness. Nobody is more pleased than me for Terry and Maurice, they deserve all the plaudits they get.

Terry's arrival was just part of the forward planning that was going on at Tannadice and the future was at the forefront of my mind that summer – little realising I would soon be taking a very different path.

25

THE POISON PEN

The two most hated men in Scottish football: the grim brothers McLean. Those were the words used to describe Jim and I in August 1998 in a newspaper article that left me shaking my head in despair. It was penned by an experienced journalist on a national paper who really should have known better. Unfortunately, for him it was all about a cheap headline and a very poor attempt to be clever.

The fact that his opinion was completely dismissed in the same article, quoting a player who had worked under both Jim and I, tells its own story. Steven Pressley presumably had been prodded to back up the caricature of my brother and I being painted in the article, but instead he was very complimentary about both of us. I'm sure the writer would argue that it provided balance to his own views on us, but I think that would be giving him too much credit. It was typical of the type of petty attack from people content to hide behind a keyboard at that time.

I have great respect for some wonderful sports writers who have been part and parcel of the Scottish game for generations. I've spoken in this book about my admiration for Jim Rodger and his incredible passion for the game and his profession. Unfortunately, there have been others who didn't come close in terms of integrity or knowledge of football. You learn to live with that, but I have to admit the talk of hatred really did trouble me. It was a deliberate attempt to play to the gallery and stoke up the flames of what was already burning away in the background in Dundee.

The fans' group United for Change was beginning to gather momentum in the 1998/99 season. The aim was to put pressure on Jim and the board to step aside, with Eddie Thompson in the background and ready to step in. Nobody at Tannadice at that time was burying their head in the sand. From top to bottom there was an acceptance that improvement was vital, but I think it is an incredible slight on the men who were in place at that time, myself included, to suggest that there had to be blood on the carpet in order for that to happen. There were individuals who had lived and breathed Dundee United for decades who were treated very poorly during that period in the club's history. That is a deep source of regret for me, and not from a personal perspective, as I had a small part to play in the grand scheme of things.

I don't think anyone would question Eddie Thompson's passion for the club, but there were some distasteful things going on in the background and it was a horrible time for everyone involved. The media were being used as a tool to unsettle the supporters and the picture was getting very blurred because of some of the statements being made and information being fed to journalists. The truth of the matter is that Dundee United was the best-run club I had ever been involved with, from top to bottom. Those involved in United for Change were looking for anything they could get their teeth into, and I hated to think I was adding to the problem for the board, so I did what I felt was the right thing. My time as manager at Tannadice ended in September 1998, two years after I had arrived.

It had been a difficult start to the season, with defeats to

Kilmarnock, Celtic and Motherwell in the new SPL. There was a draw with Hearts sandwiched in between and in the League Cup it was hard going too, with a penalty shoot-out victory against Stirling Albion and then defeat after extra-time up at Ross County. With everything that was going on off the pitch and the scrutiny the directors were coming under, I felt a huge responsibility. I felt I was letting them down and, particularly, I was letting my brother down. It was the first time in a lifetime in football that I had found myself in that situation, but I was prepared for it. All of the conversations Jim and I had before I joined in the first place came flashing back into my mind and I knew what I had to do. I'd been used to battling as a player and as a manager and never shirked a challenge, but this was one that I had to let go.

The board had a meeting and I was called to attend. I was very clear in my thoughts, I told them, 'You have a duty to Dundee United as directors. If you think a change would be beneficial you have to do that.'

I wanted them to be clear that the family tie between Jim and I had no bearing on the way forward; it was all about what was best for the club at that moment in time. With that, I left them to their discussions and within a few days the decision was made to make the change. A very amicable split was agreed and I even went to the lengths of sounding out potential successors. When you have worked to build a squad and have brought players in, you always feel a duty of responsibility when you move on. The two candidates who stood out for taking on the job at Tannadice were Archie Knox and Paul Sturrock.

Archie had not long moved to Everton as assistant to Walter Smith and, understandably, was keen to see that through, but for Paul the lure of returning to Tannadice was strong. I arranged to meet him at The Horn, the little service area between Dundee and Perth, and asked him if he would be interested in the job if it came up. He said he would, but obviously asked if I was thinking of calling it a day. I could tell him that I already had, and from then the ball was rolling.

The decision was one for the board to make, but I was at least able to let them know my own thoughts on who my successor should be, safe in the knowledge that if United were to make an approach there would be a willingness on Paul's side. I was pleased when he was eventually appointed. He had a passion for the club like no other candidate could have had. His bond with the supporters was strong too and, above all else, he had proved himself to be an astute manager with St Johnstone.

For my part, I walked away proud to have served as manager of a fantastic football club and satisfied I had done my best for Dundee United. I loved the club and I loved the city. We went from bottom of the Premier Division and candidates for relegation to third place in the table and secured European football, something that had been far from anyone's mind when I took over. We reached a Scottish Cup semi-final and League Cup final and consolidated our place in the top flight, while all the time developing some good young players in the shape of Paul Gallacher, Craig Easton, Jim Paterson and Steven Thompson. They were all positives to take from a two-year period that was eventful, to say the least.

26

A RANGERS RETURN

Forget location, location, location – try facilities, facilities, facilities. One of the biggest challenges Scottish managers and coaches have faced for generations is finding the right environment to go about their daily work. Slowly but surely, we are starting to get it right. Clubs like Hibs and Hearts have put their houses in order, although many of the provincial clubs are playing catch-up and are having to beg and borrow space simply to be able to put on training sessions.

The Old Firm, as you might expect, now have some of the best facilities in Britain at their disposal, but it wasn't always the way. In my time at Ibrox we trained at the Albion and when I moved into coaching at the club I remember having to put players through their paces in a corner of the pitch that was lit because there weren't proper floodlights. Celtic had Barrowfield, which was a far cry from their plush surroundings at Lennoxtown now.

It is crazy to think back now at the millions of pounds worth of talent that was being bought without anywhere for them to go to work, but that was the way it was at Rangers right through to the opening of Murray Park in 2001. I watched from the outside as the plans were unveiled and the complex began to take shape, and then got a very unexpected call inviting me to be part of what was happening at the new centre at Auchenhowie.

It was in March 2001 that I was first contacted, a few months before the ribbon was cut by Dick Advocaat and Sir David Murray himself. David himself had picked up the phone to ask whether I would be interested in returning to Rangers and working at Murray Park, something that I really didn't need to give any thought to at all. Once you have been at the club it is always part of you, and even though I had been away for almost twenty years there was still a huge attraction to me. Even setting aside the emotional attachment, I don't think any coach in the land would have needed much persuading to go and ply their trade at what was, and still is, a wonderful set-up.

I drove through to Edinburgh to discuss the offer with David, the manager Dick Advocaat and his assistant Bert van Lingen. At that stage Jan Derks held the title Head of Youth Development, but what they were offering me was the position of Director of Youth Development. Jan had a year left to run on his contract and I was asked to work alongside him for that period, with the intention being for me to go it alone after twelve months. Unfortunately that role never materialised.

For me it was a good opportunity. I hadn't been on the frontline since resigning from the manager's post at Dundee United two and a half years earlier, although I hadn't been away from football. When Alex Smith had taken over at Tannadice from Paul Sturrock in 2000 he had invited me and Paul Hegarty back onto the coaching staff, with my role primarily working with the youngsters at the club a couple of days a week. I also did a bit of scouting for Alex, as well as some radio work and acting as an SPL delegate.

I had plenty to keep me busy during that time, but the Rangers proposition represented a full-time job and the opportunity to work with some of the finest young players in Scotland. That was hugely attractive, as was the financial security it represented.

The trade-off was it meant uprooting the family from Dundee, where we were very settled, to move nearer to Auchenhowie. Beth and Lorna were both very supportive and knew it was a chance I couldn't refuse, but I know it must have been difficult for them. We started house hunting and eventually settled on a new development in Larbert, where we still live today.

The first year, with Jan still in place, was a chance for me to see how the system was working. I have to admit there were things I didn't agree with, but I was encouraged by the quality of players I could see in the pipeline. Players like Gary McKenzie, now at Blackpool, and Alan Hutton, Steven Smith, Chris Burke, Ross McCormack and Charlie Adam were among the batch coming through at that time and you could see their potential. My experience of working with Dutchmen is that they tend to be very single-minded – it's their way or no way. Jan was that type of character and I had to accept that whilst trying to piece together my own views on how the future should be shaped.

I felt the system was too centralised and that we needed a regionalised one, with quality coaches in the districts and a beefed-up scouting system to make sure Rangers were dominant not just in Glasgow but across the country. That was what I was keen to implement. I was also involved on the fringes of the link-up with Northern Spirit in Australia, the club David Murray had bought with a view to exploring football in that part of the world and looking at the potential to create a feeder team for Rangers in the southern hemisphere. It was David Murray Junior's pet project and I was detailed to look at it from a football perspective. My verdict was that I didn't think there was much scope for a fruitful relationship between Spirit and Rangers, which I don't think was the feedback the Murrays had hoped for. My involvement after that was limited and in time the Australian adventure was dropped, although I'm sure my input had no bearing on that.

Closer to home, the whole landscape changed for me less than a year after I had gone back to Rangers. In December 2001, Dick Advocaat stepped aside and Alex McLeish was appointed manager. During the initial discussions about my job I was assured it was a club appointment, rather than one at the discretion of whoever the manager was at a given time, but in practice that was difficult to carry through.

Alex came in and after my first meeting with him I could tell my own position was going to be difficult. I outlined my role in the system and my views, but all the time I felt in the long term there would be changes. I would describe our relationship as strained, stemming from the Motherwell connection. He had taken a bit of stick after coming in at Fir Park after me and for making changes too quickly, and I think he found that difficult.

It transpired that George Adams was the man lined up to oversee the youth set-up, with George coming across from Motherwell, where he had been director of football, in the spring of 2003. There could have been friction, but he was very reasonable with me and asked me to stay and lend my experience to the youth team. His plan was for me to take the Under-18 team and for John Brown, who had been working with the youngsters, to take the reserves. It made sense for me, as the most experienced coach, to take the Under-18s under my wing and I was happy to do that.

Within months of George starting his job, my own focus changed completely. Beth was diagnosed with breast cancer in May 2003 and it was another one of those moments when football pales into insignificance. So often the rock for the rest of the family to lean on, we had to be strong for Beth as she fought to get better. And she was so, so brave. After surgery and nine months of gruelling treatment, things to this day are progressing well. It was a huge relief, although anyone with experience of cancer will tell you that the worry does not stop there, it stays at the back of your mind for years to come. Ten years have passed since that diagnosis but neither of us take anything for granted – we're just incredibly grateful to the doctors and nurses who were such a great support during the treatment.

It is fair to say that my mind wasn't 100 per cent on the job, something I hope most people would understand. With the situation at home and the changes at the club, we came to an agreement to terminate my contract early. Work is important, but you have to realise where the priorities lie and there was no contest – family will always come first.

When I had joined Rangers the understanding was that it was a three-year contract, although the thought at the time was that it could well be a job for life if all things had been equal. It remains a major disappointment to me that having moved from Dundee to Larbert, Rangers reneged on the original agreement and my role of Director of Youth Development never materialised. However, had I not moved on from Murray Park I would have missed out on some of the most enjoyable and rewarding years I have had in coaching, and I have my old Kilmarnock teammate Ross Mathie to thank for those.

I worked under Ross in the Scotland set-up from 2006 to 2011 and can quite honestly say I loved every minute. Initially I'd been scouting for him, but it was when I began coaching that I really got bitten by the bug again. Donald Park had been assisting Ross, but Donald moved to Caley Thistle to take up the assistant manager's job under John Roberston. Gardner Speirs had also been involved before moving on to concentrate on the manager's job at Queen's Park. That created an opportunity that was perfect for me. We were working with the teams in the sixteen to eighteen-years age groups, a brilliant time to get players, as they are still young enough to learn but old enough to take responsibility.

I was one of the team supporting Ross, with Jim Clark coaching and John Ritchie working with the goalkeepers. We also had Brian Ewing, the sports scientist, as well as Les Donaldson, who was the education officer for the boys when they were away from school due to international commitments. Each had an important role to play and it was a wonderful group to be involved with, a great atmosphere. Of course, it helped that we had the cream of the crop in terms of players to work with. For me as a coach that was a breath of fresh air, having spent the bulk of my managerial career fighting to get my hands on quality players to improve my teams.

With Scotland you're guaranteed to be working with the country's best talent, and there were many who came through during that period who impressed me greatly. Kris Boyd, still at Kilmarnock then, was a predatory striker even at a young age. Danny Wilson, John Fleck and Jamie Ness were evidence of Murray Park starting to pay dividends, whilst the Aberdeen pair of Fraser Fyvie and Jack Grimmer were real talents, as was Celtic's Islam Feruz. Matthew Kennedy, another Killie youth product, also shone.

The common denominator shared by all of those players is that they have since chosen to pursue their careers in England, a real loss for the club scene in Scotland. While we will never stop that talent drain, primarily due to the financial gulf between the two countries, I do think we have to be taking a closer look at how we cater for young players in that transitional phase.

While people line up to take kicks at the state of youth development in Scotland, I maintain that we actually do a very decent job in bringing through teenagers in this country. Where it has fallen down in recent years has been giving those same players the opportunities between eighteen and twenty at club level to really kick on and fulfil the potential they have displayed up to that point.

In the most recent season, 2012/13, the SPL clubs did show encouraging signs of offering youngsters opportunities of first-team starts, certainly more than they did in the five years prior to that. Until recently managers had been reluctant to embrace the Under-21 player rule in the SPL. Personally I think introducing regulations to force clubs to field youngsters in their squad was a good thing, leaving it to chance is never going to work because of the huge financial strain every club is under in the current climate. Managers are paying high wages to squad men and feel they don't get the benefit if they don't put them on the bench. By stipulating two, Under-21s have to be part of the match-day squad, on the bench as a minimum, the dilemma is being lifted from the shoulders of the managers.

In saying that, I do think the coaches and managers have to take the initiative more often. There have been opportunities in recent years – particularly at Rangers and Celtic – where teams have been in a commanding position but have still not taken the opportunity to blood youngsters. If you can't do it when the pressure's off, when will you do it? Jimmy Johnstone, Willie Henderson, Alex Edwards, Jocky Scott and I were all blooded at sixteen years old. The big question is whether these young wingers would get that chance if we had broken through in this generation rather than our own.

I have to admit I don't think we would have got the same opportunity, as managers today aren't inclined to take a gamble on a rookie. They don't take a chance on the hopeful player that might do a job. Nine times out of ten it will be the established squad player, the safe option, who gets the nod. Again, a lot of it boils down to the fact that they are having to pay those squad players their first-team wages and have to justify that by playing them. The pressure is so intense I can understand why it happens.

That intensity isn't necessarily helping with the quality of the product at club level. I attend many matches now as an SPL delegate and can watch with impartiality. I've asked myself many times how the standard today compares with that of my own playing days and the years in which I was managing in the Premier Division. In my opinion the calibre has dropped whilst all around us we see other leagues and countries developing at pace.

All the talk of reconstruction has been well intentioned, but as long as the clubs can act with self-interest at the forefront of their minds then we are never going to get a solution that truly benefits football at all levels in Scotland. The challenge is for the governing bodies to take a firm stance and make tough decisions for the long-term benefit of Scottish football. Time is ebbing away and there has to be swift and decisive action before it is too late and our club sides fall further behind on the European stage and the international team slips further as a result. There has to be a common purpose instead of the divisions we have seen in recent years, divisions which have only served to compound existing problems in our game.

Some of the issues are actually in society rather than football itself, but we have to find ways around those. We have all lamented the demise of street football, with a tendency to look back with rose-tinted glasses to the good old days. If you boil it down, what we've actually lost is the touches of the ball that street football gave youngsters who grew up in the jumpers-for-goalposts era. The SFA's development teams for many years have been working hard to put a modern twist on it, particularly with the introduction of four-a-side football at the youngest age groups and the transition to seven-a-side after that. I do still worry that the pitches are too big and that kids aren't seeing enough of the ball as they have to, if we're truly going to allow them to progress.

We have to continue to work hard on coach education for those young age groups. The volunteers who keep the boys' clubs and school teams running are worth their weight in gold, but they can't be expected to hold the answers. You have to have people who have played at the very highest level available to advise and to shape policy for our juvenile clubs to follow.

Kids have to be given freedom to express themselves, but even at a young age we can be making a big difference to how the future of our game takes shape. It is all about instilling good habits at an early age – those habits are in passing, control and movement. If you can't pass the ball, you're not going anywhere; if you can't control the ball, you're always chasing. When it comes to passing ability, it isn't only about accuracy. It is about the effectiveness of that pass. Penetrating the opposition defence is the aim, so going forward is the priority – but only if you are in control of that forward pass. If you're not, the next option is to go square; that's saying to your teammate, 'I can't go forward, can you?' If you can't go square, we have to be telling our young players that it is acceptable to go backwards and start again. It is all about keeping control of that football. Simple stuff, but sometimes it gets lost or overcomplicated.

The bottom line is we need to have good youngsters coming through to fill the void each and every year. In saying that, it is the same with supporters. We need more youngsters watching the game as well as playing it; otherwise the club game will die off. In that respect, I'd advocate standing areas for families and room for the little ones to wander around – anything to prevent them losing interest altogether and being lost to the game.

I don't think anyone is in any doubt that we need to revitalise football in this country and no stone should be left unturned. The balancing act is making sure we don't lose sight of the many good things that are going on in the sport. I do think we can be overcritical as a nation.

It was when Mark Wotte was appointed to the role of performance director of the SFA in 2011 that Ross Mathie decided it was time to retire. He was sixty-five at that stage and it was the right time for him to go. When Ross went, we all decided to leave at the same time and make a clean break. It just wouldn't have been the same without us all together.

Everything I have seen and heard since has reinforced in me that it was the right decision to make. I don't believe it is a happy camp at Hampden in the youth set-up, where already three coaches have walked away from their positions, and I'm far from convinced by some of the rhetoric I've heard from Wotte. It appears to be a case of imposing the Dutch system in Scotland, without perhaps fully appreciating the strengths that we have here. The Netherlands have not dominated international football, so it is not a blueprint that we should accept without questioning the way the theory translates into practice. We have our own traditionally Scottish traits that we have to embrace, not least a competitive spirit that I know Dick Advocaat was very envious of after he experienced it at first hand at Rangers.

We have to take that competitiveness and really make it count. It is no different to being a joiner – whatever it is you do in life, you should want to be the best you can be. For some players ambition may mean playing in the top flight, for others it may be making the international team; for some it might be to go on and play for one of Europe's big clubs. It is different for everyone, dependant on ability, but the bottom line is that everyone needs ambition to drive them on. What I saw in the teenagers we were working with over a lengthy period was a real fire in the belly and a hunger to succeed, something Mark Wotte and his new coaching team will already be benefiting from.

I did smile to myself when I read an interview recently in which he reeled off a list of young Scots he felt would make it right to the top. I counted six out of nine who had been brought through by Ross, so the old system must have been doing something right. Wotte certainly talks a good game and has said he should be judged after ten years, which sounds like the type of contract everyone in football would like. What is it they say? You can fool some of the people some of the time, but not all of the people all of the time.

There have already been huge changes in the budget for the youth set-up, which in itself is not a bad thing. The priority has to be in ensuring it is being spent wisely and the return on investment is demonstrated. There has to be accountability and a sense that things are improving rather than just changing for the sake of change. The ultimate goal is to produce more players who are capable of competing on the international stage with the full Scotland team, and I've seen at first hand the level we are aiming for.

While working with the SFA I had an unexpected return to the senior international fold when George Burley asked me to join his backroom team in 2008. I'd had George in my team at Motherwell and had always got on well with him; we were on the same wavelength in terms of the way we liked to play the game. Still, it was a pleasant surprise when I got the call from him. What I was asked to do was watch the internationals from the stand, with a particular emphasis on the opposition team. I'd then report back to George at half-time with my observations and he could use that to shape his own decisions or to build into his team talk at the interval.

It was a challenge I relished, a really interesting brief, and it showed a lot of foresight on George's part. As a manager you tend to get wrapped up in what your own team is doing, the good and the bad, and often you can miss important facets of the opposition's tactical approach. Pulling that together in the space of forty-five minutes and then distilling it into a very short debrief in the dressing room made it an interesting job to do, but I think it worked well. Having another set of eyes in the stand, where above all else there's a better vantage point than when you're down on the touchline, was a good innovation and it shows the lengths George was going to in order to improve things.

I was desperately disappointed for him when it didn't work out, and not because of my own involvement. I was a small part of his team and would only join up with them on the eve of the match for a briefing session to prepare for the game itself. I did do some additional scouting of the opposition teams too, but it was Terry Butcher and Steven Pressley who were the coaches on the ground.

Having worked with Terry at Dundee United I thought it was a very shrewd appointment by George. I couldn't for the life of me understand those who were up in arms about the prospect of an Englishman being involved with the national team, particularly given his experience at that level. The two of them had also played together at Ipswich under Bobby Robson, so had been very well schooled by a master and a gentleman. Steven, who was new to coaching, was brought in to bridge the gap between the players and the senior coaches and it gave him good experience before he stepped into the manager's chair at Falkirk.

Ultimately the Scotland job is results driven, but I think we've seen since George just how difficult it is at present. He was given a very difficult time and had a lot to contend with during his time in charge; realistically once you have lost the support of the media then it becomes an impossible role to fulfil.

We have fallen off the pace at international level and have a lot of ground to make up, but I'm not one of the doomsayers who think we will never make it back. There are plenty of talented young players out there. We just have to make sure we nurture them properly and give them the best possible chance of progressing.

27

THE LAST WORD

Whether it's a muddy training field, a rain-soaked dugout or a windswept stand it is very difficult to replicate the adrenalin rush football provides when you're in the thick of it. When I'm asked whether I miss that direct involvement, I never hesitate to say 'yes'. Because I've been away from the Scotland set-up for a couple of years now, I think there's an assumption that I retired at the same time as Ross Mathie. While I haven't actively been pursuing jobs, I certainly wouldn't rule out a return in some capacity. I do some work now as an SPL delegate, attending games as an observer, but that is no substitute for getting the sleeves rolled up and being in the middle of it all.

In saying that, experience has taught me that sometimes it is better to take a step back and be realistic. I have had opportunities in the club game, but I haven't been willing to jump feet first if it isn't right for me. The highest profile offer was to go in and manage Kilmarnock after Jim Jefferies had left in 2010. They were in a real fight for survival, down at the wrong end of the SPL table, and the chairman, Michael Johnston, was looking for somebody to come in and rally the troops for the battle.

I was over in Malta with the Scotland youth team when I got the call from Killie. I'll always have a soft spot for the club. It was where my journey in football began and Rugby Park holds many happy memories for me. Because of that, I was naturally interested in listening to what they had to say.

Ross Mathie was insistent that I should fly back immediately rather than delay, so I left with his blessing and entered into talks with Michael. I went into those discussions hoping to be persuaded, but the more I listened the more I began to realise it wasn't right for me. What I was being asked to do was to come in for a short burst, for four to six games as a caretaker manager to buy them some time. Of course, the incentive was that if I'd done well I would have been in pole position for the job on a permanent basis, but I didn't think it was fair to judge over the course of what would have been a couple of months, at most, to get through a fixture backlog.

I had to let my head rule my heart and decline the invitation, as much as it pained me to do so. On the flight back from Malta, my mind was racing. I was already planning ahead and I'd said to myself that I would look to take Jim Clark in to assist me if it all worked out.

I'd seen enough of Kilmarnock to know they had a squad good enough to stay up, it was just a case of a change of approach and a freshening up after a long period under Jim's stewardship. He had assembled a good bunch of players who for whatever reason were underachieving that season.

In the end it was the time limit that put me off. I told Michael he would find it difficult to get anyone to work on the basis he was proposing and that proved to be the case. When he eventually made an appointment it was through to the end of the season rather than for a shorter period, which was what I'd suggested in the first place. Jimmy Calderwood was the man who came in and he managed to keep them up before moving on, opening the door for Kenny Shiels to come in.

I'm wise enough to know that SPL jobs don't come along too

often and it would have been very easy to grab that opportunity with both hands, regardless of the nagging doubts I had. When I look at the success Kenny had at Kilmarnock, winning the League Cup in 2012 in particular, I could be forgiven for wondering what might have been if I'd given it a go myself, but I actually haven't once wished I'd made a different decision. It would have been very different if I had been out of the game at the time, but it cropped up at a time when I was engrossed in the Scotland work with Ross and his teams. I could have been giving all of that up for the sake of managing back in the SPL for a couple of months, then found myself back on the outside looking in at the end of it.

Of course I've taken a step back since Ross retired, but I'm the first to admit I miss the buzz of being involved day to day. There's life in the old dog yet and if the right role reared its head I'd certainly be keen to get involved again.

I think sometimes my experience counts against me. Chairmen and directors can have a perception because of my CV that I'd only operate at a certain level, when in fact my motivation now is very different from five years ago, ten years ago or twenty years ago. At my stage it is very much about the right challenge, whether that is in youth development – a real passion of mine – or working with senior teams. At Rangers I cut my teeth coaching the likes of Billy Davies, Davie McPherson, Derek Ferguson, Ian Durrant and Robert Fleck on windswept nights at the Albion. I've followed their careers ever since. At Motherwell I had Tam Boyd, Jim Griffin, Chris McCart, Phillip O'Donnell, Andy Walker and Fraser Wishart, amongst many others, under my wing. The work we did overhauling the youth policy provided the foundation for the Scottish Cup success, a source of great pride. At Dundee United I was pleased to be able to help Scott Gallacher, Jim Paterson, Craig Easton and Steven Thompson on their way.

They were the latest to roll off a conveyor belt at Tannadice that has been producing for decades, a great example that many other clubs followed. With Scotland's youth teams I was able to help the finest individuals from clubs the length and breadth of Britain come together to form some excellent teams, all driven by the pride in the dark blue jersey. As a coach, it was a thrill to be involved. Each scenario was very different, but throughout it all, I have always got a real kick from seeing young players making the most of the talent they have.

It is no different when it comes to working with young coaches and managers – the aim is exactly the same: to help give them a fighting chance of success. Ideally it would be great to support a new manager in a similar way Alex Smith has done at Falkirk in recent years. I certainly feel I have a lot to offer given my experience and I'd be comfortable passing that on. The problem is that experience can be seen as a threat and I can understand why a young manager might be reluctant if their chairman suggested that type of set-up. I do think it can work, though, as long as the boundaries are clear and the intentions are good.

After a lifetime in the game and everything I've been through on and off the pitch, the good times and the bad, I'm a far better and stronger person. And one thing's for sure, I'm not ready to write the final chapter quite yet.